Build Stronger Teams, Make Better Decisions, and
Lead With Confidence

LISTENING *louder*

Why the Best Leaders Talk Less and Achieve More

JOEL GREIG

LISTENING LOUDER

Why the Best Leaders Talk Less and Achieve More

ISBN: 979-8-994855-1-5 (Paperback)

Library of Congress Control Number: [To be assigned]

First Edition: February 2026

Published by Joel Greig

Oceanside, California

www.joelgreig.com

Cover design by Joel Greig

Bulk purchasing: Special discounts are available on quantity purchases by corporations, associations, and others. For details, contact joel@joelgreig.com.

Printed in the United States of America

lis·ten·ing loud·er | *'lis(ə)niNG 'loudər*

verb phrase

1. The practice of creating more influence through intentional silence than through speech; prioritizing the act of deeply hearing others over the impulse to be heard.
"The best leaders master listening louder—they understand that their silence gives their team permission to think, grow, and own solutions."
2. Leadership approach characterized by asking questions instead of providing answers, pausing before responding, and making space for others' voices to emerge and strengthen.
"When she started listening louder, her team's engagement scores doubled within three months."
3. The paradoxical discovery that reducing one's own talk time increases one's actual influence and impact on team performance.
"Listening louder transformed him from a manager who solved problems to a leader who developed problem-solvers."

JORDAN'S TEAM

A Quick Reference

NAME	ROLE	KEY TRAITS & DEVELOPMENT
JORDAN VALE	Team Manager	Promoted for expertise, learning that leadership requires different skills. Journey: developing people vs. solving problems.
Marcus	Senior Account Mgr	Strategic thinker, experienced. Learning to trust his own instincts vs. defaulting to Jordan's direction.
Sofia Reyes	Top Performer	Data analyst. Exit interview reveals Jordan never listened—her departure catalyzes his transformation. Returns when culture changes.
Taylor	Operations Lead	Execution expert, organized. Resists change but reveals strategic thinking capability—sees systems, not just tasks.
Devon	Innovation Lead	Creative, energetic. Discovers hidden leadership capability beyond just generating ideas.
Kevin	Newest Member	Quiet, analytical. Seems "adequate" until Jordan listens for potential—reveals sophisticated systems thinking.
Jamal	Team Member	Steady contributor. Benefits from Jordan's leadership transformation.

Key Mentors

Sam		Jordan's mentor. Retired executive who learned "listening louder" through his own journey. Teaches through questions, not answers.
Alex Martinez		Peer manager. Her team's superior performance triggers Jordan's wake-up call. Recommends Sam; later reconnects with Sofia.

"The leader who talks the most often listens

the least."

CHAPTER 1: THE MONDAY MORNING MEETING

Jordan Vale arrived at Conference Room B seven minutes early, laptop already open, agenda color-coded on the screen. Monday morning team meetings were sacred—the rhythm that set the week's tempo. Jordan believed in starting strong.

By 9:00 AM, all six team members had filtered in. Jordan smiled warmly, making eye contact with each person.

"Good morning, everyone! Hope you all had a good weekend. Let's dive in—lots to cover but I want to hear from all of you today. Three priorities: the Henderson account, Q2 projections, and the website redesign. Marcus, tell me where you are on Henderson."

Marcus pulled up his notes. "I've been working on the proposal, and I think we could really differentiate ourselves by leading with our innovation framework. Henderson's industry is being disrupted, and I noticed in their annual report that their CEO mentioned wanting to stay ahead of changes. They're worried about becoming obsolete. I think if we position ourselves as the partner who helps them innovate rather than just cut costs, we'd stand out from every other firm pitching them the same efficiency story."

"That's interesting," Jordan nodded enthusiastically. "Innovation angle, I like that you're thinking strategically. Here's what's been rolling around in my head—these folks are pretty traditional, right? Conservative firm, been around forty years. So while innovation matters, I wonder if we're better off emphasizing stability first. Show them we can reduce costs and streamline operations, then layer in the innovation piece as the bonus. Does that resonate? Lead with what keeps them up at night—the bottom line."

Jordan was already sketching on the whiteboard. "What if we structured it like this: cost savings and ROI up front, implementation timeline in the middle, then innovation and future-proofing at the end? Strong close, right? Leaves them excited. And pull the Westfield case study—that one's a home run every time. Draft by Wednesday work for you?"

Marcus looked at his notes, then back at Jordan. "Sure, I can do that."

"Perfect. Sofia, let's talk Q2 projections. What are you seeing?"

Sofia opened her spreadsheet, a hint of excitement in her voice. "Okay, so I've been analyzing patterns from last quarter, and there's something really interesting happening with our subscription renewals. The timing seems to correlate with our email campaign frequency in a way I haven't seen before. When we send campaigns on a bi-weekly schedule, renewals jump by nearly twelve percent compared to monthly sends. I built a whole model tracking this across different customer segments, and the pattern holds even when I control for seasonal variations. I think we might be able to use this to predict renewal rates more accurately and maybe even optimize our campaign timing."

"Email campaigns, yes! That's good data," Jordan leaned forward. "Did you remember to account for the seasonal dip we get every March? That always throws projections off. Last year that March dip caught us off guard. We need to be smarter this time."

Jordan pulled up a document on the shared screen. "I sent out that new forecasting template last month—are you using that? It's got the seasonal adjustments already built in, plus leadership loves the format because it's consistent across all departments. I love that you're being thorough with your own model, but let's use the template as the foundation. You can always add supplementary analysis, but this way we're all speaking the same language when we present upstairs. Make sense? Plug your numbers into that framework and let's review Thursday. I'm really curious about this email campaign correlation you mentioned—we can definitely explore that."

Sofia's energy dimmed slightly. "Okay."

"Jamal, website redesign. Talk to me."

Jamal straightened in his chair. "The design team sent three mockups, and I've been thinking we should get team input since we all interact with clients differently. I noticed option one—the clean, minimalist design—actually aligns with the feedback we got from that user experience survey where clients said our current site feels overwhelming. They specifically mentioned wanting to find information faster without all the bells and whistles. Plus, a lot of our client base is in rural areas with bandwidth limitations. The minimalist approach would load quickly and give them exactly what they need without the flash. I know it's less visually exciting, but I think it might actually serve our audience better."

"Yes! Great that you're thinking about user feedback." Jordan pulled up the designs on screen. "Let me see these."

Three distinct homepage concepts filled the monitor—one minimalist, one bold with video, one information-dense.

Jordan studied them, nodding. "These are all solid. I see why you like the minimalist one—definitely clean. Here's my thought, though: we need to capture attention faster in today's environment. Option two, with the video header, creates immediate engagement. All the data I've been reading says video content drives conversion rates up by twenty percent or more. First impression is everything. Good point about bandwidth, but we can compress the video file. Technology has come so far—streaming is pretty universal now. Imagine a new client landing on our site and immediately seeing a thirty-second clip of our team in action, real testimonials, maybe some dynamic graphics. It's memorable."

Jamal glanced at the minimalist design on screen. "I suppose we could test both and see which performs better with actual users."

"Let's go with option two. We can always iterate later, but I think this is the direction that positions us as modern and professional." Jordan made a note. "Tell the design team, ask them to tighten up the color palette to match our brand guidelines, and let's aim to launch end of next month. Aggressive timeline, I know, but it'll keep momentum going. I'll run interference if you hit any roadblocks with other departments. You've got this."

Jamal nodded slowly, closing his notebook.

"Taylor, how's the client onboarding process coming?"

Taylor set down her pen. "It's going okay. I'm working through the flowchart you wanted, but I got stuck on the approval chain for international clients. The process seems to vary depending on the region and the type of services involved. Like, European clients have different data privacy requirements than Asian clients, and that changes who needs to review what. I wasn't sure if we should have separate paths for each region or try to create one universal process with decision points. Also, when there are both regulatory issues and contract modifications happening at the same time, I couldn't figure out the sequence from the documentation we have."

"Oh, perfect timing—I actually mapped that out last week." Jordan shared the screen, which filled with an intricate diagram of boxes and arrows. "I couldn't sleep one night and just started working through all the scenarios. See? Domestic clients follow the blue path, international follows red. Clear decision tree at each stage. Legal reviews everything international before it hits contracting. Domestic goes straight to contracting unless the deal's over fifty thousand, then it loops back to legal. I tried to think through every scenario. Any edge cases, just flag them for me and we'll work through it together. But this structure should cover ninety percent of situations. Finish the flowchart using this framework and I think you'll find it flows pretty naturally."

Taylor studied the diagram, her expression uncertain. "Okay."

"Devon, you've been quiet over there. How's everything going? You're, what, three weeks in now?"

Devon, the newest team member, sat up straighter. "Almost four weeks. It's going well. I finished all the training modules, and I've been learning the client database system. Actually, I found a feature in the reporting module that might help with the monthly reports we do. Right now everyone seems to be pulling data manually and building their reports from scratch, but there's an automated report builder that can pull most of those standard metrics with just a few clicks. I tested it with last month's data and it would have saved probably three or four hours of work. I wasn't sure if there was a reason we weren't using it, or if people just didn't know it was there."

"That's fantastic that you're exploring the system!" Jordan beamed. "Proactive learning—that's exactly what we need. Let me send you a video tutorial I created a few months ago. It covers the advanced features most people don't discover on their own. Really useful shortcuts that'll help you navigate everything. Seriously, Devon, if you need anything at all, my door's always open. I want you to succeed here."

Devon nodded. "Okay, thanks."

Jordan scanned the room. "Anyone else? Questions, concerns, anything I can help with?"

Marcus exchanged a brief glance with Sofia. The room stayed quiet.

"Alright, we're in good shape then." Jordan felt satisfied—the team was aligned, everyone had direction. "One more thing before we wrap. Customer satisfaction scores. We dropped two points last quarter. Not a crisis, but we can do better. I spent some time analyzing the feedback, and response time keeps coming up. So I put together a new response protocol that I think will really move the needle. Tier-one inquiries answered within two hours, tier-two within four hours, tier-three by end of business day. I've categorized common question types into tiers—the chart's in your inbox."

Sofia raised her hand slightly. "Should we maybe talk about whether those timeframes are realistic given our current workload? We're already pretty stretched, and adding stricter deadlines might create more stress without actually improving the quality of our responses. Sometimes taking a bit longer means we can give more thorough answers that actually solve the client's problem instead of just meeting a time quota."

"I based it on industry best practices," Jordan said reassuringly. "And honestly, I think once we get into the rhythm, it'll feel natural. It might be tight at first, but we're capable of this level of excellence. Look, I have confidence in all of you. These aren't random ideas—I've done the homework. Let's try it for a month and see where we land. Fair?"

Murmurs of agreement circled the table.

"Excellent. Really solid start to the week, everyone. You all know your next steps, and I'm here if you need me." Jordan closed the laptop with a satisfied click. "Let's make it a great week."

The team gathered their belongings and filed out, most checking phones immediately. Jordan stayed behind for a moment, reviewing notes, already planning Wednesday's check-in.

Twenty-eight minutes—efficient. Everyone contributed. Clear direction established. Team supported.

Outside the conference room, Jordan didn't notice Sofia's slight head shake as she walked with Marcus. Didn't hear Jamal say quietly to Taylor, "Did any of our ideas actually make it into the final plan?" Didn't see Devon pull up his notes about the database feature, hesitate, then close the file with a small sigh.

Jordan felt energized. This was what good leadership looked like—listening to the team, offering guidance, clearing obstacles. Collaborative but decisive.

The phone buzzed with a meeting reminder. Jordan grabbed coffee and headed out, already thinking through talking points for the next commitment.

Behind them, Conference Room B sat empty, chairs slightly askew, the morning sun streaming through the blinds onto a whiteboard filled with Jordan's handwriting.

CHAPTER 2: THE UNEXPECTED COMPARISON

The coffee in Jordan's hand had gone cold, forgotten during the last forty-five minutes of budget review. Wednesday afternoon stretched into that sluggish post-lunch zone where concentration required effort. Jordan stood to stretch, glancing out the office window at the parking lot below.

Movement caught their eye—a group walking toward the building's west entrance, animated conversation visible even from the third floor. Alex Martinez walked in the center, nodding while others gestured enthusiastically. Jordan recognized the faces. Alex's team.

Something about the energy intrigued Jordan. They looked like people who'd just won something.

Jordan checked the time. Two-fifteen. The quarterly planning sessions were happening all week in the large conference rooms. On impulse, Jordan headed downstairs.

The door to Conference Room A stood slightly ajar. Jordan slowed, then stopped. Through the gap, Alex sat at the head of the table, twelve team members arranged around the oval surface. Unlike Jordan's efficient group of six, Alex managed one of the larger teams—more people, more complexity, theoretically more chaos to wrangle.

Jordan leaned against the wall in the hallway, far enough back to avoid being obvious but close enough to observe.

"Okay, so we've got three options on the table." Alex's voice carried a relaxed confidence. "Priya, you mapped out the phased approach. Talk us through the pros and cons as you see them."

Priya, a senior analyst Jordan recognized from company events, stood and walked to the whiteboard. "The phased approach gives us flexibility. We implement the core features in Q2, gather user feedback, then roll out advanced features in Q3 based on what we learn. The downside is it takes longer to realize the full value, and we risk losing momentum between phases if something else becomes a priority."

"Appreciate the balanced view," Alex said. "What does everyone think? Does the flexibility outweigh the timeline concern?"

A younger team member spoke up immediately. "I think it does, especially given what happened last year when we rushed the CRM rollout. We had to backtrack and fix so many issues that we probably would've been faster doing it in phases from the start."

"Fair point," another voice chimed in. "But I'm worried about the momentum thing Priya mentioned. Remember the workspace redesign? We did phase one and then phase two got deprioritized for like eight months. We were stuck in this weird half-finished state."

Alex wrote "momentum risk" on a notepad. "So how do we mitigate that if we go phased? Anyone have ideas?"

Jordan watched as three people started talking, then laughed and deferred to each other. A woman in a blue sweater won the floor. "What if we commit the resources upfront? Like, actually block the calendar and assign the team for both phases before we even start phase one? Make it harder to deprioritize later."

"Build it into the initial project charter," someone else added. "Executive sign-off on the full timeline, not just the first phase."

Alex nodded, writing. "That's good. Marcus, you've been quiet. Thoughts?"

Marcus—different Marcus than Jordan's team member—leaned back in his chair. "I keep coming back to David's all-at-once proposal. Yeah, it's riskier, but the integration benefits are real. If we do it in phases, we're maintaining two systems simultaneously for months. That's a hidden cost we're not really accounting for."

"Say more about that," Alex prompted.

"Training, for one thing. We train people twice instead of once. Documentation has to cover both old and new processes during the transition. Support tickets get complicated because we have to figure out which system someone's using before we can even help them. It's death by a thousand cuts."

Jordan noticed how Alex let the silence sit after Marcus finished. Five seconds. Ten. People shifted, thinking.

Finally, Priya spoke again. "That's actually a really good point I hadn't fully considered. Maybe we need a hybrid? Core infrastructure all at once, but optional advanced features rolled out as people are ready?"

The room erupted in overlapping conversation. Alex didn't intervene, just watched as team members debated, built on each other's ideas, poked holes in logic. Jordan glanced at the clock. This single discussion had been going for twelve minutes. Twelve minutes on one decision point.

Eventually, Alex raised a hand slightly and the room settled. "I'm hearing a potential hybrid approach taking shape. Who wants to take a first pass at sketching what that might look like?"

Three hands went up.

"David, you're closest to the whiteboard."

"Leadership isn't measured by how much you say, but by how much others grow."

\- Joel Greig

David stood and started drawing boxes and timelines. As he worked, others called out suggestions. "Move that to phase one." "What if we flipped the order?" "Can we do those in parallel?" David incorporated the ideas in real-time, the diagram evolving into something collectively owned.

Jordan realized their neck was getting stiff from standing. How long had this meeting been running? They checked their phone. The session had started at one-thirty. Forty-five minutes on what appeared to be a single agenda item.

Yet the team showed no signs of fatigue. If anything, they leaned forward in their chairs.

Alex studied the whiteboard. "This is solid work. What's missing? What haven't we thought about?"

Another pause. Jordan felt the urge to fill it, to offer the obvious next steps, but Alex simply waited.

"Budget," someone finally said. "We've been talking about approach but not cost differences between these options."

"Yes! Thank you." A different voice. "The hybrid probably costs more upfront than phased but less than all-at-once. We should run the numbers."

"Who wants to own that analysis?" Alex asked.

Two people volunteered. Alex looked at them. "Want to partner on it?"

They nodded at each other.

"Great. Have something rough by Friday's check-in so we can pressure-test the assumptions together." Alex made a note. "What else?"

"Risk assessment," another team member offered. "Each approach has different failure modes. We should map those out."

"Good. Who's got capacity for that?"

The meeting continued, Alex orchestrating rather than directing. Jordan noticed the pattern now—Alex asked questions, created space, let silence do work. When Alex did speak, it was often to reflect back what they'd heard or to highlight connections between ideas.

"So if I'm understanding correctly, you're saying the training cost isn't just financial but also an opportunity cost because it pulls people away from revenue-generating work during the transition. Is that right?"

"Exactly."

"And that concern applies regardless of which approach we choose, so we need to factor it into all three options."

"Right."

Jordan had never seen anything like it. This wasn't chaos—there was clear structure. But the structure served to unlock thinking rather than constrain it. Alex had maybe spoken fifteen percent of the total words in the room, yet maintained complete control of the direction.

The meeting wrapped at three o'clock. Ninety minutes. Jordan's Monday meeting had covered three times as many topics in a third of the time.

Yet as Alex's team filed out, the energy was palpable. People walked in pairs, still talking, still engaged. One person was sketching something on a notepad while walking. Another pulled out their phone to schedule a follow-up conversation.

Jordan heard fragments as the group passed the hallway.

"...really think the hybrid approach solves both problems..."

"...glad Marcus brought up the support ticket thing, I hadn't thought about that..."

"...can't wait to see the budget analysis, that'll tell us a lot..."

Alex emerged last, laptop bag over one shoulder. Jordan straightened, suddenly feeling like they'd been caught eavesdropping.

"Jordan! Hey." Alex smiled warmly. "How's your week going?"

"Good, yeah. Just finished up a budget thing." Jordan gestured vaguely toward the stairs. "Saw your meeting was wrapping and thought I'd say hi."

"Glad you did. We're working through our Q2 planning—trying to nail down this implementation approach. Good group in there." Alex's tone was casual, proud but not boastful.

"Seems like a lot of debate," Jordan said, fishing.

"Best part of the job." Alex adjusted the bag strap. "When they're debating, they're thinking. When they're thinking, they own the outcome. Makes my life easier downstream."

Jordan laughed, though something uncomfortable stirred beneath the surface. "How do you keep things moving, though? I mean, that was what, ninety minutes on one topic?"

"More like two topics—we covered the implementation approach and started on vendor selection. But yeah, we go deep." Alex paused. "I used to try to speed things up, you know? Keep the pace brisk, make efficient decisions. Then I realized I was just making fast decisions that my team had to fix later because they hadn't really bought in or thought through the implications. Slow down to speed up, turns out."

The words landed with more weight than Alex probably intended.

"Anyway, I've got to run—meeting with finance in ten. Let's grab coffee soon, yeah? Would love to hear how your team's doing."

"Definitely," Jordan said.

Alex headed down the hallway, checking their phone. Jordan stood still, mind churning.

Back upstairs, Jordan's office felt different. Quieter. The list of action items from Monday's meeting sat on the desk—Marcus drafting the Henderson proposal per Jordan's structure, Sofia plugging numbers into the template, Jamal moving forward with website option two, Taylor building the flowchart based on Jordan's diagram.

All good things. Clear direction. Decisions made.

So why did Jordan suddenly feel unsettled?

They pulled up the team's latest engagement scores—the quarterly survey results that had come through last week. Jordan's team: 72 out of 100. Solid. Respectable. Not concerning.

On impulse, Jordan searched for Alex's team scores.

89 out of 100.

Jordan stared at the number. Seventeen points. That wasn't a small gap. That was a different league.

The comment section told the story:

"Alex really listens to our ideas and helps us develop them."

"I feel trusted to make decisions and take ownership."

"Best manager I've ever had—challenges us to think but doesn't micromanage."

Jordan closed the window and tried to refocus on email. But the image lingered—Alex sitting back while the team leaned forward. Asking questions while others provided answers. Creating the space that somehow produced both engagement and results.

Outside the window, clouds gathered over the parking lot. Jordan's reflection stared back from the darkening glass, coffee mug suspended halfway to their lips.

What if fast and efficient wasn't the same as effective?

The thought felt disloyal to everything Jordan believed about leadership.

But it wouldn't go away.

"Leadership is not about being in charge. It's about taking care of those in your charge."

— Simon Sinek

CHAPTER 3: THE NUMBERS DON'T LIE

The quarterly business review started at nine sharp on Friday morning. Jordan arrived early, claiming a seat in the middle of the executive conference room where he could see both the presentation screen and the faces of senior leadership. These meetings were part celebration, part accountability—teams that performed well got recognition, teams that struggled got support, and everyone left knowing exactly where they stood.

David Chen, the VP of Operations, opened with the standard overview. Revenue trends, market conditions, strategic priorities for the coming quarter. Jordan had heard versions of this speech a dozen times. He checked his phone under the table, responding to a quick message from Marcus about the Henderson proposal.

"Now let's look at team performance metrics," David said, and Jordan's attention snapped back to the screen.

A massive spreadsheet appeared, color-coded and ranked. Twelve teams listed vertically, eight performance categories spread horizontally. Green cells indicated top quartile performance, yellow meant mid-range, red flagged concerns.

Jordan's eyes went immediately to his own team's row, about two-thirds down the page.

Yellow. Almost entirely yellow, with a few greens scattered through.

Client satisfaction: 78%. Yellow. Project completion rate: 84%. Yellow. Revenue per employee: $287K. Yellow. Employee engagement: 72%. Yellow. Innovation index: 6.2 out of 10. Yellow.

Nothing red. Nothing to be ashamed of. Solidly middle of the pack.

Jordan told himself this was fine. Expected. His team was good.

Then his eyes drifted upward on the spreadsheet.

The top row blazed green like a traffic light giving enthusiastic permission.

Alex Martinez - Team 7.

Every single cell. Green.

Client satisfaction: 94%. Project completion: 97%. Revenue per employee: $412K. Employee engagement: 89%. Innovation index: 8.9 out of 10.

Jordan felt his jaw tighten.

The second row looked nearly identical.

Vanessa Zhou - Team 11.

Client satisfaction: 92%. Project completion: 96%. Revenue per employee: $398K. Employee engagement: 87%. Innovation index: 8.7 out of 10.

David was talking, his voice cheerful. "I want to call out two teams in particular who are really setting the standard this quarter. Alex, Vanessa—exceptional work across every dimension. Not just hitting targets but redefining what's possible. Let's give them a round of applause."

The room clapped. Jordan joined in, the sound of his own hands coming together feeling hollow.

Alex, sitting three seats to Jordan's left, smiled modestly and gave a small wave. Vanessa, across the table, nodded her thanks. Neither looked surprised or particularly excited. They looked like people who expected this outcome.

"Alex, want to share what's working for your team?" David asked.

Alex shifted in her seat, glancing at the spreadsheet. "Honestly, I can't take much credit. The team owns these results. I think what's made the difference is creating space for them to solve problems together. We spend a lot of time in collaborative planning, and I've been trying to step back and let solutions emerge from the people closest to the work. They're brilliant—I just try not to get in their way."

Several people around the table nodded approvingly. Jordan kept his expression neutral.

David smiled. "Leadership through trust. Love it. Vanessa, anything to add from your side?"

Vanessa considered for a moment. "Similar approach, really. I've been focusing on asking better questions rather than providing answers. When someone brings me a problem, I'm trying to coach them to their own solution instead of solving it for them. It takes longer up front, but they grow faster and I get time back on the backend because they're not coming to me for every decision."

"Outstanding," David said. "Models worth learning from, folks."

The meeting moved on. Other teams presented updates, discussed challenges, outlined plans for the next quarter. Jordan participated when appropriate, nodding at the right moments, making brief comments about his team's steady performance and upcoming initiatives.

But his mind stayed locked on that spreadsheet.

Seventeen points higher in engagement. Thirteen percent better project completion. Over $100K more revenue per employee.

These weren't small gaps. This was a different level of performance entirely.

Jordan had always prided himself on competence. His teams delivered. Projects got done. Clients were satisfied. He worked hard, stayed on top of details, cleared obstacles for his people.

So why was his solid, professional performance sitting in a sea of yellow while Alex and Vanessa floated above in green?

The meeting ended at ten-thirty. People clustered in small groups, refilling coffee, chatting about weekend plans. Jordan gathered his notebook and laptop, preparing to escape back to his office.

"Jordan, got a second?"

He turned. David Chen stood behind him, reading glasses pushed up onto his head.

"Of course."

"Walk with me." David gestured toward the hallway.

They moved away from the conference room, David's pace unhurried. He didn't speak until they'd rounded the corner into a quieter corridor.

"Your team's doing solid work," David began.

Jordan waited for the "but." It didn't come.

"I mean that genuinely. Consistent, reliable performance. I never worry about your projects falling through the cracks."

"Thanks," Jordan said, unsure where this was heading.

David stopped walking and faced him. "Here's my question. What would it take to move from solid to exceptional?"

The question hung between them. Jordan's first instinct was to list tactical improvements—better project management tools, additional headcount, clearer KPIs.

But David's expression suggested he was asking something deeper.

"I'm not sure," Jordan admitted. "I saw the numbers. Alex and Vanessa are operating at a different level."

"They are." David leaned against the wall. "You know what's interesting? Three years ago, Alex's numbers looked a lot like yours. Good, competent, middle of the pack. Then something shifted. Her results started climbing and haven't stopped."

Jordan's competitive instinct flared. "What changed?"

"You'd have to ask her," David said. "But from my observation? She stopped trying to be the smartest person in the room. Started making her team the smartest group in the building instead."

The words echoed what Jordan had witnessed on Wednesday. Alex barely speaking, the team animated and engaged, solutions emerging collectively.

"Vanessa made a similar shift around the same time," David continued. "They actually mentor each other, I think. Different styles, same philosophy—leadership is about multiplication, not addition."

Jordan nodded slowly, processing.

"Look, I'm not criticizing your approach," David said. "You're effective. But I think you have another gear you haven't accessed yet. Just something to consider." He clapped Jordan on the shoulder. "Have a good weekend."

David headed toward the elevators, leaving Jordan alone in the hallway.

Back in his office, Jordan pulled up the full performance data on his computer. The spreadsheet expanded to show trend lines over the past eight quarters.

His team's numbers were flat. Consistent, yes. But unchanged. A straight line hovering in the acceptable range, quarter after quarter.

Alex's team showed a different pattern entirely. Three years ago, David was right—her scores had been nearly identical to

Jordan's current performance. Then, starting about ten quarters back, a steady climb. Each quarter slightly better than the last. The trajectory was unmistakable.

Vanessa's chart told the same story, the inflection point occurring around the same time.

Jordan opened a new browser tab and pulled up the internal org charts, looking at team composition. Alex managed twelve people across mixed experience levels—three senior, five mid-level, four junior employees. High complexity.

Jordan managed six people, all mid-level or above. Lower complexity, theoretically easier to coordinate.

Yet Alex's results were dramatically better.

He clicked back to the engagement scores and read through the detailed comments for Alex's team.

"I've grown more in the past year than my previous five years combined."

"Alex challenges me to think bigger and trusts me to execute. It's incredibly motivating."

"Best team culture I've experienced. We solve problems together instead of waiting for direction."

"I feel heard and valued. My ideas matter."

Jordan switched to his own team's comments.

"Jordan is knowledgeable and responsive."

"Clear direction, good support when we need help."

"Meetings are efficient."

"Jordan works hard and expects the same from us."

Nothing negative. Also nothing that made his chest swell with pride.

Knowledgeable. Responsive. Efficient.

These were fine qualities. Good qualities.

But they weren't inspiring anyone.

Jordan leaned back in his chair, staring at the ceiling tiles. The fluorescent lights hummed their constant background frequency.

He thought about Monday's meeting. His team presenting ideas—good ideas, thoughtful ideas—and Jordan redirecting each one toward his own solution. Marcus wanting to lead with innovation for Henderson. Jordan choosing cost savings instead. Sofia discovering patterns in renewal data. Jordan steering her toward the template. Jamal recommending the minimalist design based on actual user feedback. Jordan selecting the video option based on general industry trends.

Every single time, his team had offered something worth considering. And every single time, Jordan had listened just long enough to formulate his own better answer.

Had he ever actually implemented one of their ideas unchanged?

The question made him uncomfortable.

His phone buzzed. A text from Marcus: "Henderson proposal draft ready for your review."

Jordan opened the attached document. The structure was exactly as he'd outlined on Monday—cost savings first, implementation timeline second, innovation as the closer. Westfield case study prominently featured. Professional, polished, persuasive.

Completely Jordan's approach with Marcus's execution.

He scrolled back to Marcus's original pitch from the meeting. Innovation framework, positioning as a partner in transformation, addressing the CEO's stated concerns about disruption.

It wasn't a bad idea. Actually, it was pretty good.

So why had Jordan dismissed it so quickly?

Because he knew better? Because he had more experience? Because his approach was proven?

Or because he simply preferred his own thinking?

Jordan closed the proposal and opened a new document. He started typing.

"Questions to consider:

- How often do I implement my team's ideas vs. my own?
- When was the last time someone on my team said something that changed my mind?
- Do my people come to meetings hoping to contribute, or expecting to be directed?
- What would happen if I talked less?"

He stared at the questions, feeling exposed by his own words.

Outside his office, the Friday afternoon energy was building. Voices carried down the hallway, people wrapping up work before the weekend. Someone laughed. A door closed.

Jordan thought about Alex's team filing out of that conference room on Wednesday, still debating and building on ideas ninety minutes after the meeting started. The energy, the ownership, the genuine engagement.

Then he thought about his own team leaving Monday's meeting, checking their phones before they'd even cleared the doorway. Taylor's uncertain expression. Devon closing his file about the database feature. Jamal's quiet acceptance when his design recommendation was overruled.

The numbers didn't lie.

Yellow wasn't good enough.

Not when Jordan knew green was possible.

He picked up his phone and scrolled to Alex's number. His thumb hovered over the call button.

What would he even say? "Teach me to be a better leader?" "Why is your team better than mine?" "How do I stop being so good at having all the answers?"

Jordan set the phone down.

But the spreadsheet stayed open on his screen, that top row of green cells glowing like a challenge he couldn't ignore.

CHAPTER 4: THE OBSERVATION

Monday morning arrived with the weight of unfinished business. Jordan had spent the weekend replaying that spreadsheet, those green cells burning into his thoughts during a run, over coffee, while pretending to watch a movie Sunday night.

The questions he'd typed Friday afternoon remained unanswered on his laptop.

By ten o'clock, Jordan found himself walking past Conference Room C on the way back from getting water. Through the glass walls, he spotted Alex and Vanessa sitting at opposite ends of a long table. Between them, representatives from at least four different departments—marketing, finance, operations, IT—maybe fifteen people total.

The cross-functional planning session. Jordan had forgotten it was happening today.

He slowed his pace, then stopped. The door stood slightly open for airflow.

Jordan had no real reason to be here. But nobody had closed the door either.

He stepped closer, positioning himself where he could observe without being obvious.

Vanessa was speaking. "So we've got three potential launch dates on the table—June fifteenth, July first, or mid-July after the conference. Each has different implications. What are we not seeing?"

A woman from marketing raised her hand. "Budget timing. If we go June fifteenth, we're pulling from Q2 funds. July first or later means we're in Q3 budget cycle, which actually gives us more flexibility because the Q3 allocation is larger."

"Okay, so budget flexibility favors the later dates," Vanessa said, writing on the whiteboard. "What else?"

"Market timing," someone from operations offered. "Our competitors are all launching in May or June. If we go July, we lose first-mover advantage."

"Or," another voice countered, "we learn from their mistakes and come in with a better product."

Alex, who hadn't spoken yet, leaned forward slightly. "Say more about that. What could we learn?"

The man from IT adjusted his glasses. "User feedback, for one. They'll hit the market, customers will respond, we'll see what works and what doesn't. Plus, their launches will reveal their pricing strategy. We could position ourselves more strategically."

"So there's a trade-off," Alex said. "First-mover advantage versus informed positioning. How do we think about that trade-off given our specific situation?"

Silence settled over the room. Jordan watched people actually thinking, not just waiting for their turn to talk.

Finally, the women from marketing spoke again. "I think it depends on our confidence level. If we're certain our product is superior, go early and dominate. If we have any doubts, the extra time to refine based on market response is worth more than being first."

"That's a clear framework," Vanessa said. "So the question becomes—how confident are we?"

Hands went up around the table. Vanessa pointed to a younger guy Jordan didn't recognize.

"Honestly? I'm about seventy-five percent confident. The core features are solid, but the user interface still feels clunky in testing. We're getting there, but I wouldn't call it superior yet."

"Appreciate the honesty," Alex said. "Anyone else want to weigh in on confidence level?"

Three more people spoke. Answers ranged from sixty to eighty percent. Nobody claimed complete confidence.

Jordan noticed what wasn't happening. Neither Alex nor Vanessa had offered their own opinion. They guided, questioned, reflected back what they heard—but didn't advocate for a specific direction.

"So we're hearing sixty to eighty percent confidence," Vanessa summarized. "Given that, what's the smart move?"

"Take the extra time," the marketing woman said. "Launch July first. Gives us two more weeks to polish the UI, and we'll have at least some early market data from competitors."

Heads nodded around the table.

"Anyone see a fatal flaw in that logic?" Alex asked.

More silence. People looked at each other, considering.

"I don't love giving up first-mover advantage," the operations guy said. "But I can't argue with the reasoning. If our product isn't clearly better, being first doesn't help us."

"Sounds like we're converging," Vanessa said. "July first launch, which gives us two more weeks of development time and lets us see initial market response from competitors. Show of hands—who can support this direction?"

Every hand in the room went up.

"Excellent. Who wants to own updating the project timeline?" Vanessa asked.

Two people volunteered. They quickly decided to split the work—one would handle the development schedule, the other would coordinate with marketing and operations.

The meeting continued. Jordan checked his watch. Twenty-five minutes on a single decision point. But the decision had been made collectively, with buy-in from every stakeholder in the room. Nobody would leave this meeting unclear or uncommitted.

He thought about how he would have run this same meeting. Laid out the options, analyzed the pros and cons himself, made a recommendation, asked for objections. Ten minutes, max. Efficient.

Also completely different in terms of ownership.

"Next item," Alex said, checking her notes. "Resource allocation for the beta testing phase. IT says they need three full-time engineers for two weeks. Marketing wants those same engineers for the promotional video project. Finance is asking if we can do beta testing with contractors to save headcount costs. Thoughts?"

A man from finance jumped in. "The contractor idea isn't about being cheap. It's about flexibility. If we use full-time engineers and the timeline slips, we're paying for idle time. Contractors we can scale up and down."

"Makes sense from a cost perspective," the IT manager said. "But contractors don't know our systems. The learning curve eats up a lot of that efficiency. Plus, quality control is harder."

"What if we used a hybrid approach?" the marketing woman suggested. "Core testing with full-time engineers, expanded testing with contractors? Best of both worlds."

"Walk me through how that would work," Vanessa said.

The marketing woman stood and went to the whiteboard. "Week one, our three engineers run the core functionality tests—the critical paths, security protocols, integration points. They document everything thoroughly. Week two, we bring in contractors to run the broader test scenarios using those documented protocols. Our engineers supervise but aren't doing the grunt work."

"I like it," the IT manager said. "Actually, that might be better than our original plan because it forces us to create really good documentation, which we'll need anyway for ongoing maintenance."

"So we get good documentation as a side benefit," Alex noted. "What else does this approach give us or cost us?"

The finance guy calculated on his laptop. "Costs about fifteen percent more than the all-contractor approach, but probably thirty percent less than three full-time engineers for two weeks. And we reduce quality risk."

"Timeline impact?" someone asked.

"Minimal if we start the documentation now," the IT manager said. "Actually, we should be doing that anyway."

Vanessa looked around the room. "Are we comfortable with this hybrid approach? Finance, does it work for your budget constraints?"

"Yeah, I can support this."

"IT, does it give you the quality control you need?"

"Definitely. Maybe even better than the original plan."

"Marketing, does it free up the engineers you need?"

"Partially. We'd still need to negotiate timing, but this is way more workable."

"Okay, so we've solved the core conflict and maybe improved the overall approach," Vanessa said. "Who wants to own documenting this plan and coordinating the next steps?"

Again, volunteers emerged. Tasks were divided. Ownership was clear.

Jordan realized he'd been standing in the hallway for forty minutes. His water bottle had gone warm in his hand.

He watched Alex ask another question, watched the group lean in with answers, watched Vanessa draw connections between ideas that people built on. The energy in the room was focused but relaxed. People smiled. They interrupted each other occasionally, but in that enthusiastic way that meant engagement, not rudeness.

Nobody was checking their phone.

Nobody looked bored or resigned.

This was collaboration. Real collaboration, not the performative kind where everyone speaks but one person decides.

Jordan headed back to his office, mind churning.

At two o'clock, he had his own team meeting scheduled. Weekly check-in, standard agenda. But maybe this was the moment to try something different.

His team filed in right at two. Marcus, Sofia, Jamal, Taylor, Devon, and now Kevin, who'd joined last month. Seven people looking at Jordan expectantly, notebooks open, ready for direction.

"Okay, let's get started," Jordan said. His heart rate had picked up slightly. "First item is the client portal redesign. We need to make a decision on the authentication system. IT has recommended we go with single sign-on, but it's more expensive and has a longer implementation timeline. The alternative is to stick with our current username-password system but upgrade the security features. I want to hear what you all think."

He stopped talking and looked around the table.

This was it. The moment to create space, ask questions, let them solve it.

Jamal spoke first. "I think single sign-on makes sense long-term. Clients have been asking for it, and it reduces friction in the user experience."

"Okay," Jordan said, trying to channel Alex and Vanessa. "What else?"

Sofia glanced at her notes. "The cost difference is significant though. We're talking about forty thousand more over two years, plus the implementation is eight weeks instead of four."

Jordan felt the familiar pressure building in his chest. He had opinions about this. Strong opinions. Single sign-on was the right move despite the cost because it would reduce support tickets and improve client satisfaction. The ROI was obvious if you looked at the full picture.

He forced himself to stay quiet.

"What do others think?" he managed.

Taylor shrugged. "I don't know enough about the technical side to have a strong opinion."

Devon nodded agreement. "Same."

The silence stretched. Five seconds. Ten. Jordan's fingers drummed the table unconsciously.

This wasn't working. They looked confused. Waiting.

"The thing is," Jordan said, unable to hold back any longer, "if we look at the total cost of ownership, single sign-on actually saves money. Yes, it's forty thousand more upfront, but we'll reduce password reset tickets by about seventy percent based on industry data. That's probably fifteen hours a week in support time we get back. Over two years, that's way more than forty thousand in labor costs."

The team nodded, Marcus writing notes.

Jordan had meant to ask a question. Instead, he'd made the case for his preferred option.

"Plus," he continued, momentum carrying him forward, "client satisfaction scores consistently show that authentication friction is a top complaint. Single sign-on addresses that directly. So we improve the user experience and reduce costs. It's the smart play even though the upfront investment is higher."

"Makes sense," Jamal said.

"Okay, so we'll move forward with single sign-on," Jordan concluded. "Marcus, can you coordinate with IT on the implementation timeline?"

"Sure."

Jordan looked at his agenda. That had taken three minutes. In the cross-functional meeting, a similar decision had taken twenty-five minutes and resulted in a creative hybrid solution nobody had started with.

"Next item," Jordan said, trying to recapture the earlier intention. "The Q2 client survey. We need to decide what questions to include. Sofia, you've been working on this. What are you thinking?"

Sofia pulled up a document. "I drafted fifteen questions covering satisfaction, product features, support quality, and likelihood to recommend. Pretty standard stuff based on previous surveys."

"Let me see," Jordan said.

She shared her screen. Jordan scanned the questions. They were fine. Solid. But he immediately saw gaps.

"These are good," he said. "I think we should add questions about pricing perception and competitive alternatives. That data would help us understand our market position better. Also, we should ask about their decision-making process—who else was involved in choosing our solution. That's valuable for the sales team."

Sofia added notes. "Okay, so add pricing perception, competitive alternatives, and decision-making process."

"Right. And maybe reword question seven—it's a bit leading as written. Instead of 'How satisfied are you with our support team?' try 'How would you rate your support experience?' More neutral."

"Got it."

Jordan caught himself. He'd done it again. Sofia had brought work, and he'd immediately started editing and adding rather than exploring what she'd already considered.

"Actually, Sofia, walk me through your thinking on the questions you included. Why these fifteen?"

She looked slightly surprised. "Well, I based them on the last two surveys so we'd have trend data. And I tried to keep it under twenty questions total because response rates drop significantly if surveys are too long."

"That's smart thinking on the response rate," Jordan said. Was this creating space? It felt awkward. "What questions did you consider but decide not to include?"

"Um, I thought about asking about pricing, actually, but I worried it might make people focus on cost and hurt our renewal rates."

"Interesting concern," Jordan said. "Does anyone else have thoughts on whether we should ask about pricing?"

His team exchanged glances. Kevin, the newest member, spoke up tentatively. "I mean, if people are unhappy with pricing, they're already thinking about it. The survey won't create that concern. Might be better to know what they're thinking."

"True," Taylor said. "And if pricing is fine, the data would be reassuring."

Jordan felt the urge to jump in, synthesize, conclude. He bit it back.

"Sofia, what do you think based on what Kevin and Taylor said?" he asked.

"I guess they're right. We should probably include it."

"Okay," Jordan said. This felt productive, maybe? "What else should we discuss about the survey?"

Silence again. Longer this time. Uncomfortable.

Marcus glanced at the clock. Jamal studied his notebook. The energy that had been in the cross-functional meeting—that animated engagement—was nowhere in this room.

Jordan felt like he was performing an experiment that was failing in real time.

"You know what," he said, abandoning the attempt, "let's make sure we include pricing perception, competitive alternatives, and decision-maker questions. Sofia, send me the revised draft by tomorrow and I'll give it a final review before we launch it. Sound good?"

Relief flickered across Sofia's face. "Perfect."

They moved through the rest of the agenda. Jordan tried twice more to ask open-ended questions and create space for discussion. Both times, awkward silence followed by someone giving a tentative answer, followed by Jordan filling the gap with his own analysis and direction.

The meeting ended at two forty-five. Forty-five minutes for six agenda items. Efficient, focused, clear outcomes.

Also nothing like what he'd witnessed this morning.

After everyone left, Jordan sat alone in the conference room. The whiteboard showed his handwriting—action items, deadlines, decisions. All his words, his thinking, his solutions.

What had he expected? That he could suddenly change his entire leadership approach in one meeting and his team would instantly transform?

They'd been trained for years to wait for his direction. Of course they looked confused when he tried to pull back.

But Alex's team hadn't always been that way. Vanessa's team had transformed. Jordan had seen the data—their numbers three years ago looked like his numbers now.

Something had shifted for them.

Jordan pulled out his phone and stared at Alex's contact information.

This time, he didn't hesitate.

He typed: "Hey Alex, could we grab coffee sometime this week? I'd love to pick your brain about something. No rush—whenever works for you."

He hit send before he could second-guess himself.

The response came thirty seconds later: "Absolutely! Tomorrow at 3? There's a good coffee place two blocks from the office."

Jordan typed back: "Perfect. See you then."

He gathered his things and headed back to his office, the contrast between the two meetings still sharp in his mind.

He didn't know exactly what he was going to ask Alex tomorrow.

But he knew he couldn't keep leading the same way and expect different results.

The spreadsheet with its rows of yellow and green cells didn't lie.

And neither did the bored expressions on his team's faces when he'd tried and failed to create the space he'd seen Alex and Vanessa build so naturally.

"The best leaders don't fill rooms with their presence—they create space for others to shine."

CHAPTER 5: THE BREAKING POINT

Sofia Reyes had been Jordan's top performer for two years. Reliable, creative, drove results without drama. The kind of employee managers dream about—someone who made Jordan look good without requiring much effort.

Which was why the calendar notification Tuesday morning felt like a punch to the gut.

"Sofia Reyes - Exit Interview - 10:00 AM"

Jordan stared at the screen. Exit interview. The words didn't make sense together.

He pulled up his email and scrolled frantically through the last week. There it was, buried under client communications and project updates. An email from HR dated last Thursday.

"This is to inform you that Sofia Reyes has submitted her two weeks' notice, effective April 15th. Please schedule an exit interview at your earliest convenience. We've set a preliminary hold on your calendar for Tuesday, April 18th at 10:00 AM."

Jordan had completely missed it. Four days ago. Sofia had quit four days ago, and Jordan hadn't even noticed the email.

He checked his calendar history. Last week had been the quarterly review meeting, the obsessing over the spreadsheet, the observations of Alex and Vanessa. He'd been so focused on what other managers were doing right that he'd missed what was happening with his own team.

Jordan grabbed his phone and texted Sofia: "Just saw the news. Can we talk before the formal exit interview?"

Three dots appeared, then disappeared. Then appeared again.

Finally: "I think the exit interview is the right place for that conversation."

Jordan's stomach dropped.

The morning crawled by. He tried to focus on email, on the Henderson proposal Marcus had resubmitted, on anything. But his mind kept circling back to Sofia.

Why? Why would Sofia leave? Where was the warning sign Jordan had missed?

He pulled up Sofia's file. Performance reviews over the past two years—all stellar. "Exceeds expectations" in every category. Last review three months ago, Jordan had written: "Sofia is an exemplary team member who consistently delivers high-quality work with minimal supervision. A real asset to the organization."

No indication of dissatisfaction. No complaints. No red flags.

At 9:55, Jordan headed to Conference Room D where HR had set up the exit interview. Maria Gonzalez from Human Resources was already there, laptop open, sympathetic expression ready.

"Morning, Jordan. I know these conversations are never easy."

"Morning, Maria." Jordan took a seat at the small round table. The room felt too intimate for what was about to happen.

Sofia arrived exactly at ten o'clock. Professional as always—dressed sharply, carrying a notebook, face composed and neutral.

"Sofia, thanks for making time for this," Maria began. "The exit interview is really an opportunity for honest feedback that helps us improve. Everything you share is confidential and won't impact your references or future opportunities with the company. Sound good?"

Sofia nodded.

"Great. So let's start with the basics. You're leaving to pursue another opportunity?"

"Yes. I accepted a position with Meridian Consulting. I start in three weeks."

Jordan kept his expression neutral, but internally he reeled. Meridian was a competitor. Not just any competitor—their main rival for enterprise clients.

"Congratulations," Maria said warmly. "What attracted you to Meridian?"

Sofia paused, choosing words carefully. "The opportunity to grow in new directions. Take on different types of challenges. Work with a team that approaches problems differently."

Generic answers. Safe answers. Jordan recognized the diplomatic tone—the things you say when you don't want to burn bridges.

Maria asked a few more standard questions. Salary competitive? Yes. Work-life balance acceptable? Yes. Relationships with colleagues positive? Yes.

Then Maria shifted. "And what about your relationship with your direct manager? Jordan's been your supervisor for two years. How would you characterize that experience?"

Sofia's neutral expression flickered. Just for a second, something else showed through—frustration, maybe, or disappointment.

"Jordan is smart and hardworking. Very knowledgeable about the industry. He was always available when I needed help."

More diplomatic language. Jordan heard what wasn't being said in the careful phrasing.

"That sounds positive," Maria prompted. "Was there anything about the management relationship that could have been better?"

Silence settled over the small room. Sofia looked down at the notebook, then back up at Maria. Something had shifted in the energy.

"Can I be completely honest?" Sofia asked.

"Please," Maria said. "That's exactly what we're hoping for."

Sofia took a breath. "Jordan is a good person and a knowledgeable manager. But I never felt heard. Not really heard. I could say things, share ideas, express concerns—but it was like speaking into a void. The words would come out of my mouth, Jordan would nod, and then he would tell me what we were actually going to do. Which was usually what Jordan had already decided before I said anything."

Jordan felt his face grow warm. He wanted to interrupt, to defend himself, to explain. But something kept him quiet.

"Can you give me an example?" Maria asked gently.

"Sure. Just last week, I brought analysis about email campaign correlation with renewal rates. I'd spent days building a model, tracking patterns across customer segments, controlling for seasonal variations. I was excited about it—this could have helped us predict renewal rates and optimize our campaigns. I had a whole presentation ready."

41

Sofia's voice remained steady, professional, but underneath Jordan heard something raw.

"Jordan listened to maybe the first two minutes. Said 'that's good data,' and then immediately redirected me to use the standard forecasting template instead. The conversation ended with me abandoning my model and just plugging numbers into a generic spreadsheet. My actual insight—the thing I'd discovered—was never seriously considered."

Jordan's memory flashed back to Monday's meeting. Sofia presenting her findings with excitement in her voice. Jordan acknowledging it briefly before steering her toward the template he preferred.

That's what good managers did, wasn't it? Kept people aligned with company standards?

"That must have been frustrating," Maria said.

"It was a pattern," Sofia continued. "Not just with me. I watched it happen with Marcus, with Jamal, with everyone on the team. We'd bring ideas, and Jordan would listen just long enough to formulate a response that was really just Jordan's idea dressed up as if it incorporated our input. After a while, you stop trying. Why put in the effort to think critically and propose solutions if the answer is always going to be whatever Jordan already decided?"

Each word landed like a small stone thrown with precision. Jordan felt them accumulating, building weight in his chest.

"So you felt your contributions weren't valued?" Maria asked.

Sofia looked directly at Jordan for the first time since the interview started. "I felt like a highly paid assistant. Someone to execute Jordan's vision, not to contribute my own thinking. That's fine for some people. But it's not why I went to business school. It's not what I want from my career."

Jordan found his voice. "Sofia, I had no idea you felt this way. You never said anything in our one-on-ones."

"I tried," Sofia said quietly. "Multiple times. But you can't hear feedback when you're already talking over it with your own ideas."

The words hit harder than anything else Sofia had said. Because they were true. Jordan could see it now—the pattern Sofia described wasn't exaggerated or unfair. It was accurate.

Maria made notes on her laptop. "Sofia, what would have needed to be different for you to stay?"

Sofia considered the question seriously. "I would have needed to feel like my brain was valued, not just my ability to execute. I would have needed space to think, to make decisions, to be wrong sometimes and learn from it. I would have needed a manager who was genuinely curious about my perspective instead of just waiting to share theirs."

"That's helpful feedback," Maria said. She looked at Jordan. "Anything you want to ask or share?"

Jordan felt exposed, defensive, and something else—ashamed.

"I'm sorry," he said. "I truly didn't realize I was doing this. I thought I was being helpful. Providing guidance. Clearing obstacles so you could focus on execution."

"I know," Sofia said, and there was no malice in the response. Just resignation. "That's what makes it complicated. You weren't trying to shut people down. You just couldn't help solving every problem before anyone else had a chance to try."

The exit interview continued for another twenty minutes. More questions from Maria, more carefully honest answers from Sofia. By the end, Jordan had a clear picture of someone who'd been slowly suffocating under his leadership and had finally found an exit.

When Sofia left the conference room, Jordan stayed behind with Maria.

"That was rough," she said sympathetically. "But really valuable feedback."

"Is this a pattern?" Jordan asked. "Other people on my team—are they saying similar things?"

Maria chose her words carefully. "I can't share specifics from other conversations. But I'd encourage you to create opportunities for honest feedback. Sometimes the people who stay are just as frustrated as the people who leave—they just haven't found their exit yet."

Jordan nodded numbly.

Back in his office, he closed the door and sat in the dark for a few minutes. No emails. No phone. Just quiet.

Sofia's words kept echoing.

"You never heard MY ideas."

"Why put in the effort if the answer is always going to be whatever Jordan already decided?"

"You can't hear feedback when you're already talking over it."

Jordan thought about Sofia's email campaign correlation data that he'd redirected toward the template. About Marcus's innovation framework for Henderson that Jordan had overruled in favor of cost savings. About Jamal's user research supporting the minimalist website design that Jordan had dismissed for the video option.

About Devon's discovery of the automated reporting feature that Jordan had responded to by sending a tutorial video instead of asking to see what Devon had found.

Every single instance, his team had brought thinking. Real thinking. And Jordan had treated it like rough draft material for his own ideas.

He opened his laptop and pulled up the engagement survey comments again.

"Jordan is knowledgeable and responsive."

"Clear direction, good support when we need help."

Reading between the lines now, Jordan saw what he'd missed before. These weren't compliments. They were resignation dressed in professional language.

Knowledgeable—he always had the answer. Responsive—he always stepped in to solve. Clear direction—he always told them what to do.

His team wasn't praising him. They were describing someone who'd turned them into executors instead of thinkers.

Jordan checked the time. Two forty-five. His coffee meeting with Alex was in fifteen minutes.

He grabbed his jacket and keys, but paused at the door. On his desk sat a framed photo from last year's team offsite. Everyone smiling, arms around each other. Sofia stood right next to Jordan in the picture, giving a thumbs up.

Had Sofia already been frustrated then? Had Jordan missed the signs even while standing right next to her, thinking everything was fine?

Jordan left the photo on the desk and headed out.

The walk to the coffee shop took twelve minutes. The afternoon sun felt too bright, the street too loud. Jordan moved through it mechanically, his mind still in that conference room with Sofia's calm, devastating honesty.

Alex was already there when Jordan arrived, seated at a corner table with two cups in front of her.

"Got you a cappuccino," she said, gesturing to the second cup. "Hope that's okay. You looked like you could use caffeine when you texted yesterday."

"Thanks." Jordan sat down heavily. "Though I probably need something stronger."

Alex studied his face. "Rough day?"

"Rough couple of hours." Jordan wrapped his hands around the warm cup. "Sofia quit. Just had the exit interview."

"Oh no. Sofia's great. Where is she going?"

"Meridian."

Alex winced. "That stings. What happened?"

Jordan had planned to ease into this conversation. Ask casual questions about Alex's leadership approach. Maybe pick up a few tips without revealing how desperate he felt.

But sitting across from Alex, the exit interview still fresh, Jordan's carefully planned approach evaporated.

"Sofia said I never listened," Jordan heard himself say. "That I made everyone on my team feel like highly paid assistants instead of valued contributors. That I couldn't help solving every problem before anyone else had a chance to try."

Alex set down her coffee. Her expression shifted from sympathetic to serious.

"And the worst part?" Jordan continued. "Sofia's right. Completely right. I've been watching you and Vanessa, seeing how your teams perform, trying to figure out what you're doing differently. And now I know. You actually listen to your people. You let them think. You create space instead of filling it."

"Jordan—"

"I don't know how to do that," Jordan said. The admission felt like defeat and relief at the same time. "I watched you in that cross-functional meeting yesterday. I tried to copy it in my own team meeting and completely failed. My team looked confused. I felt like a fraud. And then today, I lose my best employee because I've been slowly suffocating everyone's ability to contribute for two years without even realizing it."

Alex let the silence sit for a moment. Outside the coffee shop window, people walked by with purpose and destination. Inside, Jordan felt stuck and lost.

"Can I tell you something?" Alex finally said.

Jordan nodded.

"Five years ago, I got feedback almost identical to what you just described. Not in an exit interview—worse. In a 360 review where my entire team, anonymously, said basically the same thing. That I was smart and capable but impossible to work for because I never made space for anyone else's ideas."

Jordan looked up, surprised.

"I thought I was being a good leader," Alex continued. "Decisive, knowledgeable, efficient. Turns out I was just being controlling. I didn't see it because the results were okay. Not great, but okay. And I was working my ass off, so I figured I was doing everything right."

"What changed?" Jordan asked.

"I got a mentor. Someone who'd been where I was and found a different way. He taught me that leadership isn't about having the answers—it's about unlocking other people's ability to find them."

Jordan felt something shift in his chest. Hope, maybe. Or just the smallest opening of possibility.

"I came here today to ask if you'd help me," Jordan said. "But I didn't want to admit how badly I need it. I wanted to pretend I was just curious about your approach, maybe pick up a few techniques."

"And now?" Alex asked.

"Now I'm asking directly. I need help. I don't know how to be the kind of leader my team deserves. And I'm tired of losing good people because I can't get out of my own way."

Alex smiled, but it was kind rather than triumphant. "I can't teach you everything my mentor taught me. But I can introduce you to him. If you're serious about this."

"I'm serious."

"Then let me make a call." Alex pulled out her phone. "His name is Sam Whitfield. Retired executive, does some mentoring now. Changed my entire approach to leadership. If he has capacity, I think you two would work well together."

Jordan watched Alex type a message. The coffee shop hummed with afternoon conversations, the hiss of the espresso machine, the clink of cups.

For the first time since seeing that exit interview notification this morning, Jordan felt like he could breathe.

Sofia was gone. That couldn't be undone.

But maybe the rest of his team didn't have to be.

"Transformation begins the moment

you admit you don't have all the answers."

CHAPTER 6: THE RECOMMENDATION

Alex's phone buzzed on the coffee shop table. She glanced at the screen and smiled.

"That was fast. Sam says he can meet you Thursday afternoon if that works."

Jordan felt a flutter of nervousness. "Thursday. Yeah, that works."

"He suggested the Blue Mountain Café on Fifth Street. Do you know it?"

"I can find it."

Alex typed a quick confirmation, then set her phone down. "Fair warning—Sam's not going to give you a playbook or a list of techniques. That's not how he works."

"What does he do?" Jordan asked.

"He asks questions that make you uncomfortable. He'll push you to see things you've been avoiding. And he won't let you hide behind the story you tell yourself about being a good leader."

Jordan thought about Sofia's words from the exit interview. The careful way she'd described feeling unheard, turned into an assistant rather than a contributor. There wasn't much room left to hide.

"I think I'm past the point of comfortable anyway," Jordan said.

"Good." Alex took a sip of her cappuccino. "That's actually the best place to start. Sam says transformation only happens when you're willing to be uncomfortable."

The word hung between them. Transformation. Not improvement or adjustment. Complete transformation.

"Can I ask you something?" Jordan said. "When you first started working with Sam, what was the hardest part?"

Alex laughed, but it was a laugh of recognition rather than humor. "Realizing that everything I thought made me a good leader was actually holding my team back. I was so proud of being decisive, of having answers, of solving problems quickly. Those things got me promoted. They were my strengths."

"And Sam made you see them differently?"

"He made me see that my strengths had become weaknesses in a different context. Being decisive is great when you're an individual contributor. But as a leader, being too decisive means you're making decisions your team should be making. You're developing yourself instead of developing them."

Jordan thought about the Monday morning meeting. How efficiently he'd moved through the agenda, providing solutions, clearing obstacles. Twenty-six minutes of tight leadership.

And twenty-six minutes of missed opportunities for his team to think, to struggle, to grow.

"The hardest part," Alex continued, "was learning to shut up. Sounds simple, right? Just stop talking. But when you're used to being the person with the answers, silence feels like failure. Like you're not doing your job."

"I felt that yesterday," Jordan admitted. "In my team meeting. I tried to create space like I saw you do, and it felt like I was just wasting everyone's time. The silence was excruciating."

"It gets easier," Alex said. "But you have to trust that your team can fill that space with something valuable. And at first, they won't, because you've trained them not to. You've trained them to wait for your answer."

The observation stung because it was accurate. Jordan had spent two years conditioning his team to defer to his judgment. Of course they looked confused when he suddenly tried to pull back.

"How long did it take?" Jordan asked. "Before your team started responding differently?"

Alex considered. "Honestly? A few months before I saw real shifts. There were small wins earlier—moments where someone would surprise me with an insight I hadn't considered. But the full transformation, where my team was consistently bringing solutions instead of problems? Maybe three to four months."

Given his current situation, that felt like forever. But Jordan thought about the trend lines on the performance spreadsheet. Alex's steady climb from yellow to green. Vanessa's similar trajectory.

Real change took time.

"Sam will probably tell you this," Alex said, "but I'll say it now because it helped me. You're not going to get this right immediately. You're going to try something, fail, feel stupid, and want to go back to your old way of leading. That's normal. The key is to keep trying anyway."

"Even when it feels like you're making things worse?"

"Especially then. Because you're not making things worse— you're just surfacing problems that were always there. Your team's inability to think independently didn't start when you tried to create space for them. It started when you stopped creating space two years ago."

Jordan nodded slowly. Outside the window, the afternoon foot traffic had picked up. People in business casual heading back to offices, students with laptops searching for tables, a woman walking a small dog that seemed extremely interested in a discarded wrapper.

Normal life continuing while Jordan's understanding of leadership was being dismantled and rebuilt.

"Can I tell you what gave me hope?" Alex asked.

"Please."

"About three months in, I was in a meeting and someone on my team—Michelle, she's one of my senior people now—proposed a solution to a client problem that was completely different from what I would have suggested. My instinct was to jump in and redirect her toward my approach. But I forced myself to stay quiet and let the team discuss it."

Alex's eyes lit up with the memory. "They built on Michelle's idea, refined it, addressed the weaknesses, and came up with something genuinely better than what I'd been about to propose. And at the end, Michelle looked at me and said, 'Thanks for trusting us to figure this out.' That's when I knew the work was worth it."

"Your team thanks you now?" Jordan couldn't hide his skepticism.

"Not in those exact words every time," Alex laughed. "But yeah, they tell me they feel trusted. They tell me they're growing and they bring me problems they've already solved and just want validation on. The dynamic is completely different."

Jordan tried to imagine Marcus or Jamal or Taylor thanking him for trusting them. The image wouldn't form. Because trust required space, and Jordan had never given them space to prove themselves trustworthy.

He'd given them direction instead.

"I should let you get back to work," Alex said, checking her phone. "But Jordan, seriously—I'm glad you're doing this. It takes courage to admit you need to change."

"Feels less like courage and more like desperation," Jordan said.

"Sometimes those are the same thing." Alex stood and grabbed her bag. "Sam will text you the details for Thursday. And hey, if you need to talk after you meet with him, I'm around. This process can be lonely."

"Thanks, Alex. Really. For the recommendation, for the honesty, for all of it."

"That's what colleagues do." She smiled. "Well, that's what colleagues should do. Help each other get better."

After Alex left, Jordan sat alone at the table for a few more minutes. His cappuccino had gone cold, but he held onto the cup anyway, anchoring himself in something tangible.

His phone sat on the table, dark and silent. Then he picked it up and opened a new note.

He typed: "Things I need to stop doing."

Then he listed them:

- Solving every problem before the team has a chance
- Redirecting ideas toward my preferred solution
- Filling every silence with my own voice
- Treating my team like executors instead of thinkers
- Assuming my experience means I always know better

He stared at the list. Five items that basically described his entire leadership approach.

Jordan created a second note: "Things I need to start doing."

This one was harder. He typed slowly:

- Ask questions instead of providing answers
- Create space for others to think
- Listen to understand, not to respond
- Trust my team's capability
- Be comfortable being uncomfortable

He saved both notes and stood to leave. The coffee shop had filled up while he'd been sitting there. Every table occupied, a line forming at the counter. Life moving forward.

Jordan stepped out into the afternoon sun, pulled out his phone again, and found the text from Alex with Sam's contact information.

He typed: "Hi Sam, I work with, Alex Martinez. I appreciate you taking the time to meet on Thursday. I'm looking forward to becoming a better leader. Thanks, Jordan Vale."

He hit send before he could second-guess the wording.

The response came a few seconds later: "Thursday at 3pm works. Blue Mountain Café on Fifth. Come ready to be honest with yourself. That's the only requirement. -Sam"

Jordan read the message twice.

Ready to be honest with yourself.

After today—after Sofia's exit interview, after seeing his leadership through her eyes, and after admitting to Alex that he didn't know how to do this—Jordan figured he didn't have much choice.

The honesty had already started.

Thursday would just be the next step in a journey Jordan hadn't known he needed to take until a spreadsheet full of yellow cells and one devastating exit interview had shown him the truth.

He wasn't the leader he thought he was.

But maybe, with help, he could become the leader his team deserved.

CHAPTER 7: MEETING SAM

The Blue Mountain Café sat tucked between a bookstore and a vintage clothing shop on Fifth Street, the kind of place that had probably been there for decades while the neighborhood transformed around it. Mismatched chairs, local art on exposed brick walls, the smell of fresh-ground coffee strong enough to taste.

Jordan arrived ten minutes early. He ordered a black coffee and claimed a corner table with a view of the door, then immediately second-guessed the choice. Should he have waited for Sam to arrive first? Was picking the table presumptuous?

He was overthinking this.

At exactly three o'clock, a man in his mid-sixties walked through the door. Trim build, gray hair, wearing jeans and a navy sweater that looked expensive but understated. He scanned the café with the unhurried confidence of someone who'd spent a lifetime reading rooms and people.

His eyes found Jordan, and he smiled.

Jordan stood as Sam approached. "Sam? I'm Jordan."

"Good to meet you, Jordan." Sam's handshake was firm without being aggressive. "Thanks for being on time. Pet peeve of mine when people waste each other's time with lateness."

"I appreciate you making time for me at all."

Sam gestured to the chair across from Jordan. "Mind if I grab a coffee first? I'm useless without caffeine."

"Of course."

"Changing what you do is performance.

Changing who you are is transformation."

While Sam ordered at the counter, Jordan tried to settle his nerves. He'd prepared for this meeting the way he prepared for important client presentations—notes on his phone, key points to cover, specific questions to ask. He wanted to make efficient use of Sam's time, demonstrate he was serious about this.

Sam returned with an Americano and a chocolate croissant. He tore off a piece of the pastry before speaking.

"So. Alex says you're looking to become a better leader. Tell me about that."

Jordan had his opening statement ready. "I've been managing a team of six for two years. Results are acceptable but not exceptional. I recently realized I'm not creating the kind of environment where people can do their best work. My top performer just quit, and the exit interview made it clear that my leadership style is holding the team back. I want to change that."

Sam chewed his croissant thoughtfully. "That's a nice summary. Very articulate. Now tell me what's really going on."

The response caught Jordan off guard. "I just did."

"You gave me the professional version. The explanation you've rehearsed." Sam's tone was gentle but direct. "I asked what's really going on. What are you feeling?"

Jordan hesitated. This wasn't how he'd expected the conversation to start. He'd anticipated questions about his team structure, his goals, maybe his management philosophy.

"I'm feeling like I've been doing this wrong for two years and didn't know it," Jordan said. "Like I've been hurting people I thought I was helping."

"Better." Sam took a sip of his Americano. "Keep going."

"I watched my best employee walk out the door because I never actually listened to her ideas. I've been watching other managers get better results with more complex teams while mine just executes whatever I tell them to do. And when I tried to change my approach, I failed within minutes because I don't actually know how to do anything other than provide answers and solutions."

Sam nodded slowly. "And that scares you."

It wasn't a question.

"Yeah," Jordan admitted. "It scares me. Because being the person with the answers is who I am. It's how I got promoted. It's what I'm good at. And now someone's telling me that the thing I'm best at is actually the problem."

"Who's telling you that?" Sam asked.

"Alex. The exit interview. The performance data. All of it."

"But not you."

Jordan frowned. "What do you mean?"

"You just listed external sources telling you to change. I'm asking—do you believe you need to change? Not because Alex said so or because your team member quit. Because you looked in the mirror and didn't like what you saw."

The question landed hard. Jordan thought about Monday's team meeting. The confused faces when he'd tried to create space. The way everyone had looked at him expectantly, waiting for direction, waiting for him to solve things.

The way he'd felt relieved when he stopped trying and went back to his normal approach.

"Yes," Jordan said quietly. "I believe I need to change. Because the leader I am right now is making my team smaller instead of bigger."

Sam smiled for the first time since sitting down. "Okay. Now we can actually start."

He broke off another piece of croissant. "Alex probably warned you that I don't do techniques or quick fixes. That true?"

"She mentioned it."

"Good. Because if you came here looking for five tips to be a better listener or three tricks to engage your team, you're going to be disappointed. That's not transformation. That's performance."

"What's the difference?" Jordan asked.

"Performance is changing what you do. Transformation is changing who you are." Sam leaned back in his chair. "Performance is me teaching you to count to five before you speak. Transformation is you understanding why you can't tolerate five seconds of silence in the first place. One's a technique. The other's self-awareness."

Jordan pulled out his phone to take notes.

"Put that away," Sam said.

"I want to remember what you're saying."

"You'll remember what matters. The notes are a security blanket. They make you feel like you're capturing wisdom when what you really need to do is sit with discomfort."

Jordan hesitated, then put the phone back in his pocket. His hand felt empty without it.

"Tell me about Monday's meeting," Sam said. "The one where you tried to change your approach and failed."

How did Sam know about Monday? Had Alex given him details?

Sam read his expression. "I don't know anything specific. But I know you tried something different recently because that's what people do after a wake-up call. They try to fix it immediately. And I know it didn't work because here you are, looking for help. So tell me what happened."

Jordan described the meeting. His attempt to ask questions and create space. The awkward silences. His team's confused reactions. His own inability to stay quiet for more than thirty seconds before jumping in with solutions.

"And what did you learn from that experience?" Sam asked.

"That I don't know how to lead differently. That my team doesn't know how to respond to a different approach. That changing is harder than I thought."

"Mm-hmm. What else?"

Jordan thought about it. "That I've trained my team to wait for my answers. So even when I try to pull back, they're still looking to me to fill the void."

"Good. And?"

"And that scares me because it means this isn't a quick fix. I can't just decide to be different and have everything change."

"Excellent." Sam finished his croissant and brushed crumbs from his hands. "You're starting to see the real challenge. This isn't about learning new techniques. It's about unlearning old patterns—yours and your team's. That takes time and patience and a willingness to feel incompetent while you're figuring it out."

"How long did it take Alex?" Jordan asked.

"Different for everyone. Alex was faster than some, slower than others. But if you're asking because you want a timeline, you're asking the wrong question."

"What's the right question?"

"Am I willing to commit to this even when it's uncomfortable, even when I feel like I'm failing, even when going back to my old way would be easier?" Sam's gaze was steady. "Because that's what this requires. Not three months or six months or a year. It requires however long it takes, and a commitment to stay with the process even when every instinct tells you to quit."

Jordan felt the weight of that commitment settling over him. This wasn't a project with a defined end date. This was fundamentally changing who he was as a leader.

"I'm willing," Jordan said.

"You say that now. But three weeks from now, when you've tried something and it's blown up in your face, when your team is more confused than ever, when you feel like you're making everything worse—will you still be willing then?"

"I don't know," Jordan admitted. "I want to say yes, but I honestly don't know."

Sam's expression softened. "That's the most honest thing you've said since you sat down. And honesty is where this work lives. Not in the polished professional version of events. In the messy, uncomfortable truth."

He pulled a small notebook from his jacket pocket and wrote something, then tore out the page and slid it across the table.

Jordan read it: "When did you last hear what someone wasn't saying?"

"That's your assignment for the week," Sam said. "Not to count to five or ask better questions or implement some technique. Just to notice—in your conversations with your team, with your colleagues, with anyone—what are people saying beneath their words? What are they holding back? What are they hoping you'll hear?"

"That's it?" Jordan asked. "Just notice?"

"Just notice," Sam confirmed. "Don't fix it, don't act on it, don't try to solve it. Just practice hearing what's underneath. Because right now, you're so busy formulating your response that you're missing ninety percent of what people are actually communicating."

Jordan thought about Sofia's exit interview. How much had she been trying to tell him over the past two years that he'd completely missed?

"One more thing," Sam said, standing to leave. "This only works if you're willing to be uncomfortable. Not just intellectually willing—actually willing to sit in the discomfort and not run from it. Can you do that?"

Jordan stood as well. "I think so."

"Thinking isn't enough. I need a real answer. Are you willing to be uncomfortable?"

The question hung between them. Jordan thought about his team's faces on Monday. About Sofia's resignation. About the spreadsheet with its rows of yellow cells.

Staying comfortable hadn't worked.

"Yes," Jordan said. "I'm willing to be uncomfortable."

Sam extended his hand. "Then we have a deal. Same time next week. Same place. Come prepared to tell me what you heard that people didn't say."

They shook hands, and Sam headed for the door. He paused halfway there and turned back.

"Jordan? One last thing. This is going to be harder than you think. And more valuable than you can imagine right now. Trust the process even when you can't see where it's leading."

Then he was gone, leaving Jordan standing by the table with a cold coffee and a scrap of paper with a single question written on it.

Jordan read it again. "When did you last hear what someone wasn't saying?"

He had no idea how to answer that question.

Which, he was beginning to understand, was exactly the point.

"Before you are a leader, success is all about growing yourself. When you become a leader, success is all about growing others."

— Jack Welch

CHAPTER 8: THE LISTENING PARADOX

Jordan spent the week noticing.

Or trying to.

Sam's question—"When did you last hear what someone wasn't saying?"—proved harder to answer than Jordan expected. He'd carried that scrap of paper in his pocket all week, pulling it out during meetings, during one-on-ones, even during a call with his wife when she'd mentioned her mother visiting next month.

What wasn't being said turned out to be everywhere, once Jordan started looking for it.

Thursday afternoon arrived with spring rain tapping against the café windows. Jordan got there early again, this time intentionally choosing to wait for Sam rather than claim a table. Small adjustment, but it felt less presumptuous.

Sam arrived right at three, shaking rain from his jacket. He spotted Jordan and nodded toward their corner table from last week.

"Same spot okay?" Sam asked.

"Sure."

They ordered—black coffee for Jordan, green tea for Sam this time—and settled in. The café was quieter today, just a few other customers scattered at distant tables. The rain provided a gentle white noise backdrop.

"So," Sam said, wrapping his hands around the warm mug. "What did you hear this week that people didn't say?"

Jordan pulled out his phone where he'd kept notes despite Sam's earlier instruction. He caught Sam's raised eyebrow but pressed on.

"Monday, Marcus came to my office about the Henderson proposal. He said the client had questions about our timeline. But what he didn't say—what I heard underneath—was that he was worried we'd promised something we couldn't deliver. He was asking for permission to push back on the timeline without actually asking."

"And what did you do with that?" Sam asked.

"I asked him if he thought the timeline was realistic. He admitted he didn't. So we revised it together before sending it to the client."

"How'd that feel?"

Jordan considered. "Different. Usually I would've just solved the timeline issue myself. This time I let him name the problem, and we worked through it together. He seemed relieved."

"Good. What else?"

"Wednesday, Devon mentioned he was 'fine' when I asked how he was doing. But his body language—he looked was exhausted. I asked what was going on, and it turned out he'd been staying until eight every night trying to learn our systems because he didn't want to seem incompetent by asking questions."

Sam's expression shifted. "What did you do?"

"Told him that staying late to figure things out alone was less efficient than asking questions during normal hours. That questions don't signal incompetence—they signal engagement." Jordan paused. "Then I asked what he'd been struggling with most, and we spent twenty minutes going through it together."

"Twenty minutes," Sam repeated. "Old Jordan would've done what?"

"He would have sent him a tutorial video and moved on. Five minutes, max."

"And which approach actually helped Devon more?"

The answer was obvious. Jordan had seen the relief on Devon's face, the way his shoulders had relaxed when he realized asking questions was acceptable, even encouraged.

"The twenty minutes," Jordan admitted.

Sam smiled slightly. "You're starting to see it. The paradox."

"What paradox?"

"That slowing down actually speeds things up. That investing time in people's understanding saves time on the back end. That your silence creates space for other voices." Sam set down his tea. "Let me tell you a story. Twenty years ago, I was you."

Jordan leaned forward.

"I was a VP at a mid-sized tech company. Smart, driven, always had the answer. My teams delivered results, but turnover was high. I thought that was normal—good people get poached, that's just business. Then one day, my boss called me into his office and showed me retention data. Every other VP in the company had turnover rates between eight and twelve percent. Mine was twenty-six percent."

"What did you do?"

"First, I got defensive. Argued that my team handled the hardest projects, that high turnover was the price of excellence, that some people just can't handle the pace. My boss listened to all of it, then asked me one question: 'Sam, do you want to be right, or do you want to be effective?'"

The question settled between them like a stone dropped in still water.

"I didn't have a good answer," Sam continued. "So he gave me an assignment. For one month, I couldn't offer solutions in meetings. I could ask questions, I could facilitate, I could summarize what I heard—but I couldn't solve problems. My job was to create space for other people to think."

"How did that go?" Jordan asked.

Sam laughed. "Terrible. Absolutely terrible. First meeting, I lasted maybe three minutes before jumping in with my solution. Second meeting, I made it five minutes. I was physically uncomfortable—sweating, fidgeting, desperate to fill the silence with my brilliant insights."

Jordan recognized the feeling. His own Monday meeting attempt had been the same kind of failure.

"But here's what I learned," Sam said. "The discomfort I felt in those silences? That was my ego screaming for attention. My need to be seen as the smart one, the valuable one, the one with answers. And as long as I kept feeding that need, I was robbing my team of the chance to develop their own capability."

"So what changed?"

"I got angry enough at my own incompetence that I committed to the process instead of the outcome. Stopped trying to be good at silence and just practiced being terrible at it consistently. And slowly—very slowly—I started to notice something. When I didn't fill the space, other people did. And their ideas weren't worse than mine. Sometimes they were better."

Sam's eyes held a distant look, remembering. "There was this one meeting, maybe three weeks into the experiment. We were stuck on a product launch strategy. Every instinct told me to lay out the approach I'd already mapped in my head. But I bit my tongue and asked, 'What options do we have?' Then I counted to ten in my head and stayed quiet."

"What happened?"

"One of my junior team members—kid named George, actually—suggested an approach I never would've considered. It was risky, unconventional, and honestly kind of brilliant. The team built on it, refined it, and we ended up with a launch strategy that was exponentially better than what I'd been about to propose. And more importantly, that team owned that strategy. When challenges came up during execution, they solved them without coming to me because they'd created the plan. It was theirs."

Jordan thought about his own team meetings. How much ownership did Marcus or Jamal or Taylor feel over the decisions that came out of those meetings?

Zero. Because they were all Jordan's decisions, even when he pretended otherwise.

"Here's the paradox," Sam said, leaning forward. "The less you talk, the more influence you have. Your silence gives other people permission to find their own answers. And when they find their own answers, they're committed in a way they never could be to your answers."

"But what if their answer is wrong?" Jordan asked. "What if I can see the better solution?"

"Then you ask questions that help them see it too. Or you let them try their approach and learn from it. Or—and this is the hardest one—you accept that your solution might not actually be better, just more familiar." Sam's voice was gentle but firm. "Your job as a leader isn't to have the best answers. It's to unlock your team's ability to find answers. Those are completely different jobs."

Jordan absorbed this. Everything in his training, his experience, his identity as a leader was built on being the person with answers. The thought of abandoning that felt like abandoning competence itself.

"I can see you fighting this," Sam said. "What's the resistance about?"

"If I'm not providing solutions, what am I providing? What's my value?"

"Now we're getting somewhere." Sam's expression showed he'd been waiting for this question. "Your value is in developing people who don't need you to solve their problems. Your value is in building a team that's collectively smarter than you are individually. Your value is in creating the conditions where other people's best thinking can emerge."

"That sounds nice in theory—"

"It's not theory. It's how Alex leads. It's how Vanessa leads. It's how every leader with green cells across that spreadsheet leads." Sam's tone sharpened slightly. "You want the results they're getting? You have to do the work they did. And that work starts with getting comfortable with your own silence."

The rain had picked up outside, drumming harder against the windows. Someone at another table laughed at something on their laptop. Normal life continuing while Jordan's understanding of leadership continued to crack open.

"Here's your assignment for next week," Sam said. "Run one meeting—just one—where you don't offer a single solution. Ask questions, facilitate, summarize, reflect back what you hear. But don't solve anything."

"What if they ask me directly for the answer?"

"Ask them what they think first. If they're really stuck, ask what options they're considering. If they genuinely have no ideas, ask what information would help them develop ideas. There's always a question between their problem and your solution."

Jordan felt his anxiety rising. "This feels like I'm abandoning my team. Like I'm withholding help."

"I know it does. That's your ego talking again, telling you that your help is the only help that matters." Sam's voice softened. "But real help isn't giving people fish. It's teaching them to fish. Even when teaching takes longer and feels less immediately satisfying than just handing them a fish."

"One meeting," Jordan said. "I can do one meeting."

"You'll want to jump in. Your hands will itch to solve. You'll feel like you're wasting time. Do it anyway." Sam stood to leave. "And Jordan? Don't pick your easiest meeting. Pick a real one where actual decisions need to be made. That's where the learning happens."

They shook hands, and Sam headed out into the rain, pulling up his collar against the weather.

Jordan sat for a few more minutes, watching the rain streak down the windows. One meeting without offering solutions.

It sounded simple.

It felt impossible.

But Sam's story lingered. The discomfort in the silence. The junior team member's brilliant idea. The team owning their own strategy.

The less you talk, the more influence you have.

Jordan pulled out his phone and looked at next week's calendar. Monday, nine AM. Full team meeting. Project decisions needed on three different initiatives.

He sent a calendar update adding a note to the meeting agenda: "Collaborative decision-making session."

Then he typed a private note to himself: "Ask questions. Don't solve. Trust the process."

His finger hovered over the save button.

This was going to be uncomfortable.

Which, according to Sam, meant he was finally heading in the right direction.

He saved the update and headed out into the rain.

CHAPTER 9: THE FAILED EXPERIMENT

Monday morning arrived too quickly.

Jordan had spent the weekend mentally preparing for the nine o'clock team meeting. He'd reviewed Sam's assignment a dozen times. One meeting without offering solutions. Ask questions, facilitate, reflect back. Don't solve.

Simple instructions that felt about as achievable as holding his breath for an hour.

By 8:55, his team had filed into Conference Room B. Marcus, Jamal, Taylor, Devon, and Kevin. Five people who'd been conditioned for two years to wait for Jordan's direction. Five people who had no idea they were about to be part of an experiment that Jordan was almost certain would fail.

"Morning, everyone," Jordan said, settling into his chair. His hands already felt restless. "Thanks for being here. We've got three projects to discuss today, and I want to try something different. Instead of me laying out the approach for each one, I'd like us to work through them together. Collaboratively."

Taylor glanced at Marcus. Devon looked confused. Jamal just waited.

"Okay," Marcus said slowly. "Sure."

Jordan took a breath. "First item. The Morrison account renewal. It's coming up in six weeks, and we need a strategy. Marcus, you've been the lead on this. What's the situation?"

Marcus pulled up his notes. "Morrison's been a client for three years. Contract value is about two hundred thousand annually. I got signals from their CFO that they're shopping around, comparing us to competitors. Our relationship with their main contact is solid, but there's new leadership asking questions about ROI."

Jordan's mind immediately generated a response strategy: Shore up the relationship with the main contact, prepare a detailed ROI analysis showing three-year value, offer a slight discount if needed to retain them, schedule a meeting with the new leadership to address concerns directly.

He bit the inside of his cheek to keep from speaking.

"So what do you think we should do?" Jordan asked instead.

Marcus hesitated. "Well, I thought maybe we should—" He paused, clearly expecting Jordan to jump in. When Jordan didn't, he continued. "Maybe we should reach out to their main contact and see what's driving the comparison shopping?"

"Okay," Jordan said. "What else?"

Silence.

Jordan counted in his head. One. Two. Three. Four. Five.

The silence felt like physical pressure building in his chest.

"We could put together an ROI analysis?" Taylor offered tentatively.

"Good," Jordan said. His fingers drummed the table unconsciously. "What would that need to include?"

More silence. Longer this time.

Six. Seven. Eight.

Jordan couldn't take it anymore.

"I think we need to quantify the value they've received over three years," he said, the words tumbling out before he could stop them. "Not just in cost savings, but in efficiency gains, risk mitigation, all of it. Then we should compare that to what they'd face in switching costs—implementation time, learning curve, potential disruption. Make the case that staying is the lower-risk, high-value option."

His team nodded, taking notes.

Jordan closed his eyes briefly. Thirty seconds. He'd lasted thirty seconds before solving the problem.

"But what do you all think?" he added, trying to recover. "Does that approach make sense?"

"Yeah, that's good," Jamal said.

Of course they agreed. He'd just laid out the complete solution. What were they supposed to say?

Jordan tried to regroup. "Okay, second item. The client portal upgrade. We need to decide on the timeline and phasing. Devon, you've been researching this. What are the options?"

Devon looked relieved to have something concrete to report. "I mapped out three scenarios. We could do a full upgrade over one weekend—high risk but fastest. We could do a phased approach over six weeks—lower risk but longer disruption. Or we could run parallel systems for a month while we transition—safest but most expensive."

"What's your recommendation?" Jordan asked.

Devon shifted uncomfortably. "I don't know. They all have trade-offs. I was hoping you could help me think through which one makes the most sense."

This was it. The perfect moment to ask questions that would help Devon think it through himself.

Jordan opened his mouth to ask about risk tolerance, about resource constraints, about client impact.

Instead, what came out was: "The phased approach is probably our best bet. Yes, it takes longer, but we can't risk a failed full upgrade that takes down the portal. And parallel systems are too expensive for the marginal safety benefit. Six-week phased implementation, and we'll communicate clearly with clients about the timeline."

Devon wrote it down. "Okay, that makes sense."

Jordan felt frustration rising in his throat. He was doing exactly what Sam had told him not to do. Worse, he couldn't seem to stop himself.

"Actually," Jordan said, forcing the words out, "what do the rest of you think? What factors should we consider in this decision?"

Kevin spoke up. "Budget is tight this quarter. The parallel system cost might be prohibitive."

"True," Marcus added. "And client tolerance for disruption is probably higher than we think if we communicate well."

"So phased approach?" Taylor asked.

"Sounds like it," Jamal confirmed.

Jordan noticed what had happened. They'd had a brief discussion, arrived at the same conclusion Jordan had already stated, and confirmed it back to him. It looked like collaboration. It wasn't. It was just Jordan's decision with extra steps.

The meeting continued. Third item: new client onboarding process redesign. Jordan made it almost two minutes before providing his solution. Then he caught himself, tried to pull back with questions, but by then the momentum was already established.

When the meeting ended forty-five minutes later, Jordan had a list of clear action items and next steps.

All of them based on his solutions.

His team filed out, looking neither confused nor enlightened. Just normal. Another efficient Monday meeting where Jordan had told them what to do, dressed up in slightly more collaborative language.

Jordan sat alone in the conference room, staring at his notes. He'd failed. Completely, utterly failed. The assignment had been simple—one meeting without offering solutions—and he couldn't even manage that.

He pulled out his phone and texted Sam: "Tried the assignment. Failed spectacularly. Not sure I can do this."

The response came two minutes later: "Free now if you want to call."

Jordan stepped out of the office and into the stairwell for privacy. He dialed.

Sam answered on the first ring. "Tell me what happened."

Jordan walked Sam through the meeting. The immediate impulse to solve. The physical discomfort of silence. The way he kept jumping in with answers even when he'd explicitly told himself not to.

"I made it maybe thirty seconds on the first question before I completely took over," Jordan said. "And the worst part? It felt good. Solving the Morrison renewal strategy, laying out the portal upgrade approach—I felt competent. Valuable. Like I was doing my job."

"Of course it felt good," Sam said. "You're excellent at solving problems. That's your comfort zone. What you're not comfortable with is sitting in uncertainty while other people figure things out."

"I don't understand how you did this. How did you make it through an entire meeting?"

"I didn't. Not at first." Sam's voice carried a smile. "My first attempt, I made it about two minutes. Second attempt, maybe five. It took me a dozen tries before I could get through a full meeting without solving. And even then, it was excruciating."

Jordan leaned against the stairwell wall. "So I'm not uniquely terrible at this?"

"You're exactly as terrible as everyone is when they first try to change a deeply ingrained behavior. The difference between people who transform and people who don't isn't that the successful ones find it easy. It's that they keep trying even when it's hard."

"But my team—they were just waiting for me to tell them what to do. They didn't jump in with ideas or solutions. They just sat there."

"Because you've trained them to sit there," Sam said. "Two years of you providing answers has taught them that thinking isn't their job. You can't undo that conditioning in one meeting. They need time to learn that you actually mean it when you create space."

Jordan thought about Devon's question: "I was hoping you could help me think through which one makes the most sense." Not "What should we do?" but a request for help thinking. A small but significant difference.

And Jordan had immediately provided the answer instead of helping Devon think.

"Here's what I want you to understand," Sam continued. "That discomfort you felt? That desperate need to jump in and solve? That's not a bug in the process. That's the process. You're working against yourself. Against years of identity and habit and reinforcement that says your value comes from having answers."

"So what do I do?"

"You try again. Wednesday, Thursday, whenever your next meeting is. Same assignment. Don't expect to succeed. Just notice how long you can last before you jump in. Notice what triggers you. Notice the physical sensation of resisting the urge to solve."

Jordan heard voices in the hallway outside the stairwell. Someone laughing. Normal work continuing.

"This feels impossible," Jordan said.

"Good," Sam replied. "Now you know what you're working against—yourself. Your own need to be the smart one, the competent one, the one with answers. And that's a worthy opponent. Most people never even see that opponent clearly. You're already ahead of where I was at this stage."

"I don't feel ahead. I feel useless."

"Exactly. Welcome to the learning zone. It's uncomfortable here, but it's also where growth happens." Sam paused. "Listen, Jordan. You're going to fail at this multiple times. That's not a possibility—it's a certainty. The question is whether you'll keep trying anyway. Because on the other side of these failures is a completely different kind of leadership. But you can't skip the failing part to get there."

Jordan took a deep breath. The stairwell smelled like cleaning solution and old paint. A light on the next landing flickered like it was about to go out. That's kind of the feeling Jordan had right now.

"Okay," he said. "I'll try again. Wednesday's meeting."

"Good. And Jordan? The fact that you called me frustrated instead of giving up? That tells me you're serious about this. So I'm serious about you. We'll figure this out together."

They hung up, and Jordan stood in the stairwell for another moment.

His instinct was to go back to his office, review what went wrong, create a plan to do better. Analyze and optimize.

But maybe that was the wrong instinct. Maybe the point wasn't to get better at the technique. Maybe the point was to get more comfortable with the discomfort.

Jordan headed back to his office. On his desk sat the Henderson proposal—Marcus's work, structured exactly how Jordan had specified. Good work. Competent work.

Also completely devoid of Marcus's original thinking.

Jordan opened his calendar and looked at Wednesday's meeting. Project status updates with the full team.

He typed a note to himself: "Don't solve. Just notice how long you can last. Notice what triggers you. Notice the discomfort."

Then he added: "It's okay to fail. Just fail forward."

Outside his window, clouds moved across the sky. The city buzzed with its usual Monday energy.

Jordan had failed his first real test.

But according to Sam, that meant he was finally in the right place to learn.

CHAPTER 10: QUESTIONS AND PAUSES

Thursday afternoon found Jordan back at the Blue Mountain Café, arriving with the familiar mixture of anticipation and dread that had become his weekly ritual. Rain clouds threatened overhead, promising a downpour.

Sam was already there, seated at their usual corner table. He looked up as Jordan approached.

"How'd Wednesday go?"

"Better than Monday. Worse than I'd hoped." Jordan wrapped his hands around his coffee. "Made it about four minutes before jumping in with a solution. But I caught myself doing it, which felt like progress."

"It is progress. What did you notice?"

"The silence makes me physically anxious. My heart rate goes up. I start fidgeting. And there's this voice in my head that says if I don't fill the space, I'm wasting everyone's time."

"That voice is loud, isn't it?"

"Deafening."

Sam took a sip of his tea. "Let me ask you something. When someone finishes talking to you, how long do you usually wait before responding?"

Jordan thought about it. "I don't know. A second? Maybe less?"

"Actually, most people respond in about point-two seconds. Essentially instantaneous. You know what that means?"

"That we're efficient conversationalists?"

Sam smiled. "It means we're not actually listening. We're waiting for our turn to talk. True listening requires processing time—space between what someone says and what you say back."

Jordan recognized the pattern. In meetings, during one-on-ones, even in casual conversations—he was always preparing his next point while others were still talking.

"So what's the alternative?"

"The pause," Sam said simply. "Intentional silence between their words and yours. Three seconds minimum."

"Three seconds feels like an eternity in conversation."

"I know. Let me demonstrate." Sam leaned back. "Tell me about your biggest challenge right now with your team."

Jordan decided to play along. "My biggest challenge is that they don't seem to trust that I actually want their input. They're waiting for me to tell them what to do, even when I ask for their ideas."

He finished speaking. Sam said nothing.

One second passed. Two. Three.

Jordan felt the urge to add more, to clarify, to fill the silence.

Sam finally spoke. "You used the word 'trust' just now. What would it take to earn their trust?"

The question caught Jordan off guard. The three-second pause had given Sam time to hear the specific word Jordan used and build a question around it.

"I guess... consistency?" Jordan said. "I'd need to actually follow through on creating space, not just try it once or twice and give up."

Another pause.

Then: "What gets in the way of that consistency?"

Again, a question that went deeper because Sam had taken time to think.

"My own discomfort," Jordan admitted. "It feels inefficient. Like I'm failing to do my job."

Three more seconds of silence.

"What if the discomfort *is* the job?" Sam asked.

The question landed differently than it would have without the pause. Jordan actually had space to consider it rather than immediately reacting.

"If I'm always comfortable, I'm probably not growing," Jordan said slowly. "And if I'm not growing, my team isn't growing. So yeah, maybe the discomfort is the job."

Sam smiled. "See what happened there? I gave you three seconds to process before responding. That pause let me actually hear what you said instead of just waiting to talk. And it gave you space to think more deeply about your own answers."

"It felt weird at first," Jordan admitted. "But then it felt... respectful, somehow. Like you were taking what I said seriously enough to think about it."

"Exactly." Sam pulled out his notebook and drew a simple timeline. "Here's how most conversations work. Person A talks, Person B immediately responds, back and forth. Efficient but shallow."

He drew a second timeline with small gaps. "Here's what conversation looks like with pauses. Person A talks, silence, Person B responds, silence. Slower, but exponentially a deeper conversation. Because the silence isn't empty—it's filled with thinking."

Jordan studied the drawings. "Three seconds every time?"

"Minimum. And here's the key—don't just count and then talk. Actually use those three seconds. Ask yourself: What did they really say? What am I feeling? What question would help them think more deeply?" "You may fill the space by saying, 'Okay' or 'I see', if that makes it easier" "Just don't give you full response."

Sam leaned forward. "That brings me to the second part of today's lesson. You've been learning to create space. Now let's talk about what you do after that pause—because most managers operate from a fundamental assumption that their job is to have answers. Someone brings a problem, you solve it. Someone's stuck, you unstick them."

"That's what I was trained to do," Jordan said. "That's what has gotten me promoted in the past."

"Right. But here's the shift: your job isn't to have answers. Your job is to help your team find answers. Completely different skill set." Sam drew two columns on the page. "Old Jordan versus New Jordan."

In the left column, he wrote: "Tells. Solves. Answers. Directs. Fixes."

In the right column: "Asks. Explores. Questions. Guides. Develops."

"Everything on this side," Sam tapped the right column, "starts with curiosity instead of certainty. And the primary tool of curiosity is the question."

"I ask questions," Jordan protested.

"You did with Taylor. But I bet most of your questions in team meetings are leading questions—where you already know the answer you want and you're trying to get them to say it."

Jordan thought about Monday's meeting. "Don't you think the Henderson timeline needs to account for legal review?" It was phrased as a question, but really it was Jordan stating his opinion with a question mark at the end.

"Guilty."

Sam drew a pyramid on the page with three levels. At the bottom, he wrote "Open." In the middle, "Focused." At the top, "Closed."

"Closed questions get yes/no answers. 'Should we do X?' These aren't developmental. They're just checking for agreement."

Sam pointed to the middle section. "Focused questions narrow the thinking but still leave room. 'What options exist?' 'What's the biggest risk?' These guide without dictating."

His finger moved to the bottom. "Open questions create the most space. 'What are you thinking?' 'How do you see this?' 'What would success look like?' These unlock thinking."

"So start with open questions?"

"Yes. Then narrow with focused questions if needed. Save closed questions for when you genuinely need a yes or no." Sam flipped to a new page. "Let me show you how this works. I'll be a team member. You practice asking instead of telling."

Sam shifted his posture. "Jordan, we've got an issue with the Morrison account. Their CFO wants to cut costs by fifteen percent across all vendors. If we reduce our price that much, we're barely breaking even. What should we do?"

Jordan's instinct was immediate: don't reduce the price, show them value, offer a modest reduction paired with a longer contract commitment.

But that was telling.

He took a breath. "What do you think our options are?"

"Good start. Open question." Sam resumed his worried expression. "I guess we could reduce the price, but that seems like a bad precedent. Or hold firm and risk losing them."

Jordan paused. "What else?"

"I don't know. Those seem like the only two choices—give in or hold firm."

"What would happen if we approached it differently? Not about price at all, but about value?"

"Like how?"

Jordan caught himself about to explain. Instead: "What value are we providing that they might not be considering?"

"Well, we've saved them money in other areas. We've prevented problems that would've cost them way more than our fee." Sam's expression brightened. "I guess if we quantified that, the fifteen percent reduction looks different in context."

"What would you need to build that case?"

"Data on cost savings, testimonials, comparison to what they'd pay if they had those problems..." Sam trailed off. "Actually, I could probably pull most of that together by Monday."

"And once you have that case built?"

"Then we go to their CFO with a value story instead of a price negotiation." Sam dropped character and grinned. "See what just happened?"

"I didn't give you the answer. You found it."

"Right. And when you tell people what to do, they execute your idea. When you ask questions that help them think, they own the idea. Which person is more committed to making it work?"

"The one who owns it."

Sam wrote in his notebook:

Questions that unlock thinking:

- What are you thinking?

- What options do we have?

- What would success look like?

- What concerns you most?

- What information would help?

- What's one small step we could take?

"These aren't magic," Sam said. "But they're starting points. Real curiosity beats perfect phrasing every time."

They practiced for another twenty minutes. Some attempts were clunky—questions that were obviously leading. But others opened up thinking in surprising ways.

"Here's your assignment," Sam said finally. "Tomorrow, schedule a one-on-one. Practice the three-second pause before every response. And in Monday's team meeting, try to go the first fifteen minutes using only questions."

"Fifteen minutes feels impossible."

"Six minutes felt impossible two weeks ago. You're getting stronger." Sam stood to leave. "Pay attention to who lights up when their thinking gets unlocked. That's the person who's been waiting for this kind of leadership."

Friday morning, Jordan sent Taylor a meeting invite.

At two o'clock, she knocked on his door, looking slightly wary.

"Thanks for making time," Jordan said. "I wanted to check in. How's the workload feeling?"

"It's fine. Manageable."

Jordan counted. One. Two. Three.

In those three seconds, he actually looked at Taylor. She was gripping her pen tightly. Her shoulders were raised. Fine and manageable, but her body language suggested otherwise.

"When you say manageable, what does that actually mean day-to-day?"

Taylor blinked. "I mean, I'm getting everything done. Meeting deadlines."

Pause. One. Two. Three.

"But?" Jordan prompted gently.

"But what?"

"I heard 'I'm getting everything done' and I'm wondering if there's a 'but' after that."

Taylor's grip loosened slightly. "I guess I'm working more hours than I'd like. Staying late a couple nights a week. But that's just part of the job, right?"

Jordan used the pause to resist agreeing. Instead: "What's driving the extra hours?"

"The client response protocol. The two-hour, four-hour, end-of-day deadlines. When multiple requests come in at once, it's hard to hit them all without staying late."

Three-second pause. Jordan noticed his defensiveness rising—the urge to explain why the protocol was important. He let it sit there without acting on it.

"That sounds stressful. What would make it more sustainable?"

Taylor looked genuinely shocked. "Really? You want to know?"

"Really."

"Maybe tier-two could be six hours instead of four? Or we could have a rotation where someone's designated rapid-response person each day?"

Jordan paused again. Both ideas were practical. Better than his original because they came from someone living with the consequences.

"Which one would work better?"

"Probably the rotation. More predictable."

"Okay. Want to draft a proposal? We can test it for a month."

Taylor stared at him. "Are you serious? You want me to revise the protocol?"

"You're the one managing it day-to-day. Your idea will probably work better than anything I'd design." Jordan paused, then added, "I should've asked for your input before implementing it in the first place."

Something shifted in Taylor's expression. The wariness faded, replaced by cautious optimism.

When she left, Jordan sat back. The pauses had felt excruciatingly long. He'd wanted to jump in at least a dozen times.

But Taylor had come up with a better solution. And walked out looking like someone who'd been heard.

He texted Sam: "Did the pause exercise. Painful but effective. She proposed a better system."

The response came quickly: "And now she owns it. That's the magic."

Monday's meeting arrived. His team settled into Conference Room B. Marcus, Jamal, Taylor, Devon, and Kevin.

"Morning everyone," Jordan said. "First up—we need a strategy for the client appreciation event. What are your initial thoughts?"

Silence. Then Devon spoke. "Could we do something interactive? Like workshops instead of presentations?"

Jordan's mind generated opinions about logistics, resources, what had worked in the past.

Instead: "What would that look like?"

"Maybe small group discussions where clients share challenges and we facilitate?" Devon gained confidence. "Instead of presenting at them, we create space for them to learn from each other."

"What would make that valuable for them?" Jordan asked.

Taylor jumped in. "Peer learning. They'd trust insights from other clients more than from us."

"And what would we get out of it?"

"Direct intel on their biggest challenges," Marcus said. "Better than any survey."

Jamal nodded. "Plus it positions us as partners instead of vendors. Changes the relationship."

Jordan watched the energy build. Ideas flowing, people building on each other's contributions. He'd asked four questions. They'd generated a complete strategy.

"What would we need to make this happen?"

The team listed logistics. Kevin started documenting. Taylor volunteered to draft the proposal.

Fifteen minutes had passed. Jordan hadn't offered a single solution.

And Devon—quiet Devon who usually deferred to everyone—was beaming. He sat straighter, engaged in a way Jordan had never seen before.

That's the person who's been waiting for this kind of leadership.

The meeting continued. Jordan slipped a few times—started to offer his opinion, caught himself, turned it into a question.

When the meeting ended, his team lingered, still discussing the event, building on ideas.

Jordan's phone buzzed. A text from Devon: "Thanks for running the meeting that way. Felt good to contribute."

Such a simple message. Such enormous meaning.

Then he texted Sam: "Made it fifteen minutes. Devon's idea became the whole strategy."

Sam's response: "That light is what you're after. Keep creating space for it."

Jordan looked at his calendar. Another meeting Friday.

More opportunities to ask instead of tell.

More chances to watch his team light up.

"Be strong, but not rude; be kind, but not weak; be bold, but not a bully; be humble, but not timid."

— Jim Rohn

CHAPTER 11: LISTEN FOR POTENTIAL

Jordan was reviewing quarterly performance assessments when Sam's text arrived: "Coffee shop closed for renovations. Want to meet at Riverside Park instead? Benches by the fountain at 3?"

The change in routine felt oddly appropriate. Everything else was shifting—why not the location too?

Jordan arrived at the park ten minutes early. May had brought warmth and green to the city. Trees in full leaf, flowers blooming along the pathways, the sound of the fountain creating a peaceful backdrop. Sam was already there, two coffees from a nearby cart sitting on the bench beside him.

"Figured you'd be early," Sam said, handing Jordan one. "How's the question practice going?"

"Better. I'm catching myself before I solve now, usually. The team's starting to bring me solutions instead of problems." Jordan sat down, stretching his legs. "But I'm noticing something else. Some people are thriving with this approach—Devon, Taylor, even Marcus is bringing bigger ideas. But Kevin seems... lost. It's like he doesn't know what to do with the space I'm creating."

Sam took a sip of coffee. "Tell me about Kevin."

"He's been with the team about two months. Decent work, meets expectations, but nothing remarkable. In meetings, he mostly stays quiet unless I ask him directly. And when I do ask, his contributions are usually safe, predictable. Status updates rather than insights."

"How do you feel about him?"

The question caught Jordan off guard. "I don't know. Neutral, I guess? He's fine. Not a star, not a problem. Just... adequate."

"And how do you think Kevin feels about how you see him?"

Jordan paused. He'd never considered it from that angle. "I have no idea."

"People sense how we see them," Sam said. "Especially when we see them as adequate but unremarkable. That assessment becomes a ceiling they bump up against." He shifted on the bench to face Jordan more directly. "Let me ask you something. When you listen to Kevin, what are you listening for?"

"I'm listening to what he's saying. His status updates, his questions, his concerns."

"Right. Transactional listening. You're hearing the content—the words, the information, the surface level." Sam gestured toward the fountain where water cascaded in patterns. "But there's another way to listen. Transformational listening. Where you're not just hearing what someone says, but listening for what they could become."

"I don't understand the difference."

"When you listen transactionally, you're focused on the immediate task. 'What does Kevin need from me right now? What problem is he bringing? What answer does he want?' You're listening to respond, to transact, to move on."

Sam picked up a leaf that had fallen on the bench. "Transformational listening asks different questions. 'What capability is Kevin developing? What potential am I seeing? What's the person he's becoming, even if he doesn't see it yet?' You're listening for growth, not just information."

Sam leaned back against the bench. "Let me give you a framework for this. When you're talking to someone on your team, listen for three things—I call them the Three Potentials."

He held up one finger. "First, listen for **capability potential**. What are they naturally good at that they might not even recognize? Kevin might not know he's a systems thinker—he just knows he likes puzzles. Your job is to hear the capability beneath the interest."

A second finger. "Second, listen for **growth potential**. What are they curious about? What questions do they ask when they're genuinely engaged versus just being dutiful? Curiosity is where growth lives. If someone's asking questions, they're reaching for something."

A third finger. "And third, listen for **contribution potential**. What do they care about? What would they change if they could? When people talk about what frustrates them or what they wish was different, they're often revealing the exact contribution they want to make."

"So I'm listening for what they're good at, what they're curious about, and what they care about," Jordan summarized.

"Exactly. And here's the key—you're listening for the gap between where they are and where they could be. That gap is your leadership opportunity." Sam dropped his hand. "Most managers listen to assess current performance. You're learning to listen to unlock future potential."

Jordan pulled out his phone and made a note:

Three Potentials to Listen For:

1. Capability - What are they naturally good at?

2. Growth - What are they curious about?

3. Contribution - What do they care about?

"The gap between where they are and where they could be = my leadership opportunity."

Jordan thought about his recent interactions with Kevin. Status updates on the portal upgrade. Questions about process documentation. Requests for clarification on priorities. All task-focused. All transactional.

"So I've been listening to Kevin as a doer, not a thinker," Jordan said slowly.

"Have you given him space to be a thinker?" Sam asked. "Or have you unconsciously categorized him as someone who executes rather than creates?"

The question stung because it was accurate. Jordan had mentally filed Kevin in the "solid contributor" category—competent enough to keep, not dynamic enough to invest extra development time in.

"I've written him off," Jordan admitted. "Not consciously, but yeah. I don't see him the way I see Devon or Marcus."

"And Kevin senses that. So he shows up as adequate because that's the ceiling you've set for him." Sam crushed the dry leaf in his hand, letting the pieces fall. "Here's what I want you to try. Next time you talk to Kevin, listen for potential instead of performance. Listen for what interests him, what energizes him, what he's curious about. Listen for the moments when his voice changes or his eyes light up. Those are clues to who he really is and who he could become."

"What if there's nothing there? What if he really is just adequate?"

Sam's expression sharpened. "That's your ego talking. The ego that says you can assess someone's full potential in two months of status updates. I promise you, there's more there. You just haven't created the conditions for it to emerge."

They sat in silence for a moment. A jogger passed by, headphones in, focused on their pace. A couple strolled hand in hand, laughing about something.

"I had an employee once," Sam said. "Guy named Robert. Quiet, middle-of-the-pack performer. I saw him as reliable but unexceptional. Then one day, we had a crisis with a major client. Everyone was in panic mode, throwing out ideas. Robert sat quietly for most of the meeting, then finally spoke up with an insight that completely reframed the problem. Brilliant observation. Changed everything."

"What happened?"

"I realized I'd been listening to Robert's reports for two years without ever hearing him. I'd categorized him as a quiet implementer and stopped paying attention to anything that didn't fit that category. After that crisis, I started actually listening—not just to what he said, but for what he cared about, what made him think differently."

"And?"

"He became one of my strongest strategic thinkers. Not in spite of being quiet, but because of it. He processed deeply before speaking. When he contributed, it was worth hearing. But I'd almost missed it entirely because I wasn't listening for his potential."

Jordan finished his coffee, the cup now cold in his hands. "So how do I listen for potential with Kevin?"

"Start by getting curious. Not about his task completion, but about him as a person. What draws his attention? What questions does he ask when he's genuinely interested versus when he's just being dutiful? What did he do before this job that might reveal capabilities you haven't tapped?"

Sam stood and tossed his empty cup in a nearby bin. "Your assignment: have a conversation with Kevin where you're listening for potential. Not his next task, not his performance issues, just who he is and what he cares about. See what emerges."

"That's it? Just talk to him?"

"With completely different ears than you've used before. Listen like he might surprise you. Because he will, if you create space for it."

Friday afternoon, Jordan knocked on the doorframe of Kevin's cubicle. Kevin looked up from his laptop, surprised.

"Hey Kevin, you have twenty minutes? Wanted to chat."

"Sure, of course." Kevin quickly minimized whatever he'd been working on. They walked to one of the small meeting rooms off the main floor.

Once settled, Jordan realized he hadn't planned what to say. Usually he'd have an agenda, talking points. This time, just Sam's instruction: listen for potential.

"I realized I haven't really checked in with you since you joined the team," Jordan started. "Not about tasks, but about you. How's it been going?"

Kevin looked wary. "It's going well. I think I'm getting up to speed on most processes."

"That's good. But I'm curious about something else. What drew you to this type of work originally?"

The question seemed to catch Kevin off guard. "You mean client services?"

"What aspect of it interests you most."

Kevin paused, thinking. "Honestly? I like solving puzzles. Every client situation is different—different constraints, different stakeholders, different goals. Figuring out how to navigate all those variables and create something that actually works is... satisfying."

Jordan noticed Kevin's posture had changed slightly. Less guarded, more animated.

"What kind of puzzles do you like most?" Jordan asked.

"The messy ones." Kevin's eyes brightened. "Where there's no clear right answer and you have to synthesize a bunch of competing priorities. Those are interesting."

"Give me an example from before you joined our team."

Kevin described a project from his previous company—a system integration with impossible timeline requirements and budget constraints. The way he talked about it revealed someone who thought systemically, who saw connections others missed, who thrived on complexity.

This wasn't the Kevin from team meetings who gave brief status updates.

This was someone else entirely.

"That's impressive work," Jordan said. "I'm curious why you haven't brought that kind of thinking to our team discussions."

Kevin's animation faded slightly. "I guess I wasn't sure it was wanted. Everyone seemed to have their roles. Devon's the innovator, Marcus handles complex accounts, Taylor manages processes. I'm still figuring out where I fit."

Jordan heard what Kevin wasn't saying: I don't know if there's room for my thinking here.

"What if I told you we need exactly the kind of systems thinking you just described?" Jordan said. "That ability to see connections and navigate complexity—we're actually missing that."

"Really?" Kevin looked genuinely surprised.

"Really. In fact, we've got a challenge coming up that might be perfect for you." Jordan described the client portal integration project—multiple systems, competing requirements, tight timeline. "It's a puzzle. A messy one. Want to take the lead on figuring it out?"

Kevin leaned forward. "Yeah, absolutely. I'd need to understand the technical constraints better, and I'd want to talk to the teams using each system to understand their workflows, but yeah. I could map out an approach."

"What would you need from me?"

"Honestly? Just space to dig into it. And maybe check-ins where I can test my thinking with you before presenting to the broader team."

"Done. Let's plan on thirty minutes Monday to get you started, then weekly check-ins as you work through it."

Kevin nodded, energy visible in his expression. "This is great. Thank you."

After Kevin left, Jordan sat in the small meeting room for a few minutes longer. The same person who'd seemed adequate and unremarkable twenty minutes ago had just revealed capabilities Jordan hadn't known existed.

Not because Kevin had changed.

Because Jordan had finally listened for who Kevin could be instead of who Jordan had decided he was.

Jordan pulled out his phone and texted Sam: "You were right about Kevin. There was a lot more there. I just wasn't listening for it."

Sam replied: "That's the shift. Every person on your team has more potential than you're currently seeing. Your job is to listen for it and create space for it to emerge."

Jordan looked at his team roster on his laptop. Marcus, Jamal, Taylor, Devon, Kevin. Five people he thought he knew.

How much potential had he been missing in each of them?

What would happen if he started listening to all of them the way he'd just listened to Kevin—not for what they could do for him, but for who they were becoming?

Outside the window, the afternoon sun filtered through the trees. Birds called to each other. The world continuing its patient work of growth and change.

Jordan closed his laptop and headed home, carrying with him a new question.

Not "What do I need from my team?" but "Who could they become if I listened closely enough to hear it?"

The following Monday, Jordan arrived early to find Devon already in the conference room, whiteboard covered in diagrams. The client appreciation event had become Devon's passion project.

"Morning," Jordan said, setting down his coffee. "You're here early."

"Couldn't sleep. Had an idea about the breakout sessions." Devon gestured to the board. "What if instead of us facilitating everything, we train a few clients to lead discussions? They know their industries better than we do. We could provide the framework, but they'd drive the conversation."

Jordan studied the diagram—participant flow, topic selection, facilitator training timeline. It wasn't just creative. It was strategic.

"Walk me through how you'd select the facilitators," Jordan said.

Devon's whole demeanor shifted—more confident, more animated. He described a selection process that considered industry expertise, communication skills, and willingness to experiment. He'd thought through contingencies, backup plans, follow-up engagement.

This wasn't just an idea. This was leadership.

"Devon, I'm curious about something," Jordan said. "Have you ever led a team before?"

"No. Always been the creative guy. Come up with ideas, other people execute them." Devon shrugged. "That's kind of my lane."

Jordan heard what Sam had taught him to listen for—capability Devon didn't see in himself.

"What if that's not your only lane?" Jordan asked. "What if you've been a leader without the title? Because what you just described—stakeholder management, risk mitigation, team coordination—that's leadership work."

Devon looked uncomfortable with the assessment. "I mean, I can organize stuff when I'm excited about it, but that's different from actually leading people."

"Is it?" Jordan pulled out a chair and sat down. "You got Kevin excited about the logistics complexity. You convinced Marcus that interactive was better than traditional. You've been coordinating this whole project. What do you think leadership is?"

"I guess... I thought it was about being in charge. Making the calls."

"Leadership is about creating conditions for good work to happen. You've been doing that." Jordan pointed to the whiteboard.

"This client facilitator idea—you're not trying to control the event. You're designing a system that lets the best ideas emerge. That's sophisticated leadership thinking."

Devon sat down across from him, processing. "I never thought about it like that."

"Here's what I'm wondering," Jordan said, listening for the contribution potential Sam had described. "What if you took the lead on this event—not just the creative side, but the whole thing? Project lead. You'd coordinate with Taylor on logistics, Marcus on client selection, Kevin on systems. I'd be here for questions, but it would be your call."

"That's... a lot bigger than I was thinking."

"I know. But I'm listening to how you think about this project, and I'm hearing someone who could lead it. Question is, do you want to try?"

Devon looked at the whiteboard, then back at Jordan. "Yeah. Yeah, I do."

"What would you need from me?"

"Probably weekly check-ins? And maybe help if I get stuck on the people side of things. I'm less confident there than on the creative side."

"Done. But Devon—I think you're going to surprise yourself with how capable you are on the people side. You've already been doing it. You just haven't been calling it leadership."

After Devon left, energized and slightly nervous, Jordan made another note in his phone:

Devon - Saw himself as "creative guy." Actually natural leader. Was hiding leadership capability in his innovation role. Needed permission to see himself differently.

CHAPTER 12: THE RESISTANCE

The client appreciation event planning was in full swing. Devon had taken the lead, energized by the interactive format he'd proposed. Kevin was mapping out the logistics with the kind of systems thinking Jordan now recognized. Marcus had partnered with marketing on outreach.

Everything was moving forward smoothly.

Except for Taylor.

Tuesday afternoon, she appeared in Jordan's doorway, arms crossed, expression tight.

"Got a minute?" Her tone suggested it wasn't really a question.

"Of course. Come in." Jordan gestured to the chair across from his desk.

Taylor sat but didn't relax. "I need you to make a decision about the breakout session topics for the event. Devon wants to let clients choose their own discussion topics on the day. Marcus thinks we should pre-set topics based on industry trends. They keep going back and forth, and we need to finalize this by Friday."

Jordan's old instinct kicked in immediately—he had an opinion about which approach was better. Pre-set topics would be easier to facilitate but less responsive to actual client needs. Client-chosen topics would be more relevant but harder to prepare for.

But he caught himself. This wasn't his decision to make.

"What do you think we should do?" Jordan asked.

Taylor's jaw tightened. "I think you should decide. You're the manager. That's your job."

"I'm curious about your perspective first. You've been coordinating the planning—what are you seeing?"

"A leader is one who knows the way, goes the way, and shows the way."

— John C. Maxwell

"What I'm seeing is that we're two weeks out and we don't have basic decisions made because everyone's so busy collaborating and discussing and exploring options." Taylor's frustration spilled over. "We used to be more efficient than this."

Jordan paused, caught off guard by the direct criticism. "You think the collaborative approach isn't working?"

"I think it's slowing everything down. Devon's excited because he gets to run with his idea, Kevin's in his element with the complexity, Marcus loves the strategic conversations. But someone has to actually execute all this, and that someone is usually me. And I'm drowning in indecision."

"What would help?" Jordan asked.

"You telling me what to do!" Taylor's voice rose slightly. "Like you used to. 'Taylor, here's the plan, here's your part, make it happen.' Clear, simple, efficient. Now everything's a question and a discussion and 'what do you think?' and honestly, I don't have time to think. I just need to know what we're doing so I can do it."

The words landed hard. Jordan had been so focused on creating space, on asking questions, on developing his team's thinking. He hadn't considered that for some people, that space might feel less like freedom and more like abandonment.

But something else was happening in this conversation. Jordan heard it beneath Taylor's frustration.

He was listening for potential.

Taylor wasn't just complaining about process—she was identifying a real problem. The gap between creative exploration and execution. Between collaboration and decision-making. She was seeing something important that everyone else was missing.

"I hear you," Jordan said carefully. "And I appreciate you being direct with me." He paused, then shifted gears. "Taylor, can I ask you something? You said someone has to execute all this, and that someone is usually you. Why do you think that is?"

Taylor looked surprised by the question. "Because that's my job. I'm the operations person. Devon creates, Marcus strategizes, Kevin solves puzzles. I make things happen."

"Is that how you see yourself? As the person who executes other people's ideas?"

"That's what I'm good at." Taylor's defensiveness softened slightly. "I like taking a plan and making it work. I'm organized. I follow through."

Jordan remembered Sam's framework. Listen for the gap between where they are and where they could be.

"What if I told you that what you just did—identifying the tension between collaboration and execution, seeing the decision-making bottleneck—that's strategic thinking, not just operational execution?"

Taylor blinked. "I'm just pointing out what's not working."

"You're diagnosing a system-level problem," Jordan said. "That's different from complaining. You're seeing a pattern that affects the whole team. That's strategic thinking."

"I never thought of it that way."

"What else do you see that's not working?" Jordan asked. "Not in terms of tasks, but in terms of how we operate as a team?"

Taylor hesitated, then: "Honestly? I think we've over corrected. You used to make all the decisions. Now sometimes it feels like no one's making them. There's a middle ground we're missing."

"Keep going."

"Like... maybe some decisions should be collaborative and some should be directive. Maybe the framework should be: if it's about strategic direction, we discuss it. If it's about execution details, whoever's doing the work decides. But right now everything's in the discussion bucket, even stuff that doesn't need to be."

Jordan felt something click. This was exactly the kind of thinking he needed.

"That's brilliant," he said. "That's the insight I've been missing. We need decision-making criteria."

Taylor looked genuinely surprised. "Really?"

"Really. In fact, would you be willing to draft a proposal? Decision framework for the team. When we collaborate, when we delegate, when I need to make the call. You clearly see this more clearly than I do."

"I... yeah. I could do that."

"And Taylor, I want you to know something. I've been thinking of you as our excellent executor. But you're more than that.

You're seeing system-level issues and proposing solutions. That's leadership thinking. I should have been listening for that sooner."

Taylor's expression shifted—still frustrated about the immediate problem, but something else there too. Recognition, maybe. Possibility.

"Can I still be honest about something?" Taylor asked.

"Always."

"This shift has been really hard for me. I thought I was doing good work before. Now it feels like everything I knew about working with you doesn't apply anymore, and I'm supposed to figure out new rules that nobody's explaining."

"That's fair feedback," Jordan said. "I've been changing the rules without really explaining why. And I can see how that would be frustrating and confusing."

Taylor's arms remained crossed but her posture softened slightly. "It's not just confusing. It's scary. What if I'm not capable of what you're asking? What if I'm just good at execution and that's okay?"

"Then that's okay," Jordan said. "There's nothing wrong with being excellent at execution. But I want you to have the chance to find out if there's more there before you decide." He leaned forward. "I believe you're capable of strategic thinking. You just proved it by diagnosing our decision-making problem. But I understand if you're not sure yet."

Taylor looked down at her hands. "What if I make the wrong call on something important?"

"Then we'll learn from it together. But I don't think there is a wrong decision here with the breakout sessions. Both Devon's approach and Marcus's approach have merit. The question is which trade-offs we're willing to accept. And based on what you just described about collaboration versus execution, you're as equipped to evaluate those trade-offs as I am. Maybe more equipped."

"I need to think about this," Taylor said.

"Take your time. And work on that decision framework when you're ready. I think it could really help the team."

After Taylor left, Jordan pulled out his phone and texted Sam: "Taylor just taught me about decision-making frameworks while she was complaining about my leadership. I almost missed it because I was hearing criticism instead of listening for her strategic capability."

Sam replied: "The best insights often come disguised as complaints. Good catch."

Jordan made a note in his phone:

Taylor - Saw herself as "operations executor." Actually has strategic mind that sees system gaps. Was frustrated because she thought her job was to execute, not to design. Needed to see her diagnosis as valuable contribution, not just complaining.

But he also felt unsettled. Taylor's resistance was real. Her discomfort was valid. And he wasn't sure if he'd handled it right—trying to reframe her criticism as strategic thinking when what she'd asked for was clarity and direction.

He texted Sam again: "But also—she wanted me to just tell her what to do. Did I dodge that by turning it into a development conversation?"

Sam's response: "Can you talk now?"

Jordan called.

"Tell me what else happened," Sam said.

Jordan walked through the rest of the conversation, Taylor's frustration with the collaborative approach, her request for him to just make decisions like he used to.

"And how do you feel about what she said?" Sam asked.

"Defensive at first. Like she was criticizing the whole transformation I've been working on. But also guilty, because she's right that I've changed the rules without really explaining why. And uncertain—what if she's right that we've over corrected?"

"Good self-awareness. Now let me tell you what's actually happening here." Sam's voice was calm, assured. "Taylor's not resisting collaboration. She's resisting change. And that's completely normal."

"So what do I do?"

"First, understand what you're asking of her. For two years, Taylor's job was to execute your decisions. She got good at that. Efficient at it. Probably took pride in being someone who could take direction and deliver results. Now you're asking her to think strategically, make decisions, handle ambiguity. That's a completely different skill set."

Jordan hadn't thought about it that way. "So I'm asking her to do a job she wasn't hired for."

"You're asking her to grow into a bigger version of herself. Some people are excited by that—Devon, Kevin, they're thriving with it. But others experience it as threatening. Their competence was built on the old system. The new system makes them feel incompetent, at least temporarily."

"So Taylor feels like she's failing."

"Exactly. And her solution is to go back to what worked before. Get you to tell her what to do so she can feel competent again." Sam paused. "The question is, do you let her go back? Or do you hold the space and help her grow through the discomfort?"

Jordan thought about Taylor's capabilities. She was organized, detail-oriented, excellent at execution. But was she capable of strategic thinking? Of making complex decisions?

He realized he didn't actually know. Because he'd never asked her to.

Until today. And she'd done it—she'd identified a system-level problem and proposed a framework solution.

"I want to help her grow," Jordan said. "But I don't want to lose her like I lost Sofia."

"Different situations. Sofia was being stifled—she had capability you weren't using. Taylor's being challenged—you're asking her to develop capability she hasn't needed before. The key is acknowledging the discomfort instead of pretending it's not there."

"How do I do that?"

"Talk to her directly. Not about the breakout session decision—that's just the surface. About the bigger shift and why you're making it. About your own discomfort with changing. About your belief that she's capable of more than execution, even if that feels scary right now."

Jordan absorbed this. "And if she still wants me to just tell her what to do?"

"Then you make the call on whether she's willing to grow or whether she needs a role that fits the old model. But give her the chance first. Most people will step up if you're honest about what you're asking and why it matters."

They talked for a few more minutes. Sam shared a story about an employee who'd resisted his leadership shift, then eventually became one of his strongest strategic partners. The key had been naming the transition openly instead of pretending it wasn't happening.

"You're teaching them to think," Sam said. "That's uncomfortable at first. Like learning any new skill. But the discomfort means they're in the learning zone, not the comfort zone. Your job is to normalize that discomfort, not eliminate it."

After hanging up, Jordan sent Taylor a meeting invite for the next morning. "Coffee? Want to talk more about yesterday's conversation."

She accepted without comment.

Wednesday morning, Jordan met Taylor at the same coffee shop where he'd been meeting with Sam. Neutral territory felt important.

Taylor arrived looking guarded but less angry than yesterday. They ordered—cappuccino for Jordan, Earl Grey tea for Taylor— and found a quiet table.

"Thanks for making time," Jordan said. "I've been thinking about what you said yesterday, and you're right about a lot of it."

Taylor's eyebrows rose slightly.

"I have been changing the rules without really explaining why. And I can see how that would be frustrating and confusing." Jordan wrapped his hands around his coffee cup. "So let me tell you what's been happening on my end."

He told her about Sofia's exit interview. About the performance data showing his team underperforming. About his realization that his strength—having answers—had become a weakness that prevented his team from developing their own capabilities.

"I've been working with a mentor for the past several weeks, learning a completely different approach to leadership. And honestly, it's been uncomfortable for me too. I've felt incompetent, uncertain, like I'm failing at my job most days."

Taylor's expression softened slightly.

"But here's what I'm learning," Jordan continued. "When I solve every problem and make every decision, I develop myself but

I don't develop my team. I turn you all into executors instead of thinkers. And that's not fair to you, and it's not sustainable for the team's performance."

"So the questions, the collaboration—it's not you testing us?"

"No. It's me trying to create space for you to grow into bigger roles, to develop capabilities you haven't needed before." Jordan paused. "But I get that growth is uncomfortable. And I should have been more upfront about what I was doing and why."

Taylor took a sip of her tea, considering. "It does feel uncomfortable. I liked knowing exactly what was expected. Now everything feels ambiguous."

"I know. And I'm asking you to sit in that ambiguity instead of running from it. Because on the other side of it is a version of you that thinks strategically, makes complex decisions, maybe even leads your own team someday." Jordan met her eyes. "And I already saw evidence of that yesterday. That decision framework you described? That's not executor thinking. That's leader thinking."

"What if I'm not ready for that?"

"Then we'll go at whatever pace works for you. But I want you to have the chance to find out what you're capable of." Jordan leaned forward. "Here's what I'm proposing. Let's take the breakout session decision you brought me yesterday. Instead of me deciding, I want you to work through it using that framework you described. I'll guide you, but you'll make the final call. And we'll see how that feels."

Taylor looked uncertain. "What if I make the wrong decision?"

"Then we'll learn from it together. But Taylor, I don't think there is a wrong decision here. Both Devon's approach and Marcus's approach have merit. The question is which trade-offs we're willing to accept. And you're as equipped to evaluate those trade-offs as I am."

They spent the next twenty minutes walking through the decision. Jordan asked questions—What's most important to our clients? What's most important to the team? What's the worst-case scenario for each approach?—and let Taylor work through her thinking out loud.

By the end, she'd landed on a hybrid: pre-set topics for half the breakout sessions, client-chosen topics for the other half. Best of both approaches.

"That's actually better than either original option," Jordan said. "You just created a third path nobody else had thought of."

Taylor smiled, cautiously. "I guess I did."

"How did that feel?"

"Scary. But also... kind of good? Like I actually contributed something instead of just implementing someone else's idea."

"That's the shift. And it gets less scary the more you practice it." Jordan finished his coffee. "I'm not going to stop asking you what you think. But I'll try to be clearer about why I'm asking and what I'm looking for. Deal?"

"Deal." Taylor stood to leave, then paused. "Jordan? I'm sorry about yesterday. The 'just tell me what to do' thing. That wasn't fair."

"You were honest about how you felt. That's exactly what I need from you." He paused. "And I'm serious about that decision framework proposal. I think it could really help the whole team understand when we collaborate and when we delegate. Will you work on it?"

"Yeah. I will."

Walking back to the office separately, Jordan felt something settle. Taylor wasn't fully on board yet—that would take time. But she was willing to try. Willing to sit in the discomfort instead of demanding a return to the old way.

And more importantly, she'd revealed strategic capability that Jordan had never asked her to use before. He'd been so focused on her execution excellence that he'd missed her systems thinking entirely.

He texted Sam: "Talked to Taylor. I think we're okay. She made a great decision on her own. And she's going to draft a decision-making framework for the team."

Sam replied: "The resistance you faced was part of the process, not a deviation from it. Well navigated. And it sounds like you heard her strategic thinking beneath the frustration."

Jordan pocketed his phone and kept walking, the morning sun warm on his face.

Encouraging individuals to engage in critical thinking was uncomfortable.

For them, and for him.

But uncomfortable was where growth lived.

And sometimes the loudest complaints contained the quietest insights.

CHAPTER 13: REFLECTION AND PRESENCE

The Thursday mentoring session had become the anchor of Jordan's week. A chance to step back and make sense of what was happening.

Sam suggested they walk instead of sitting. "Better thinking happens when you're moving," he said.

They strolled along the riverside path, early June heat softened by shade from overhanging trees.

"How are things with Taylor?" Sam asked.

"Better, I think. Less resistant. But something's still off. Like there's a gap between us that wasn't there before."

"What kind of gap?"

"Trust, maybe? Or connection. She's doing what I ask, but it feels transactional. Like she's going through the motions without fully buying in."

Sam nodded. "That's common after a confrontation, even a productive one. You addressed the surface issue, but there's probably something deeper she hasn't said. Maybe something she doesn't even recognize herself."

"So how do I find out what that is?"

"You listen for it. And when you hear it, you reflect it back." Sam paused at a bench. "It's called the echo effect."

He pulled out his notebook. "Most people think listening is about staying quiet while someone talks. But real listening has a second step—showing the person you actually heard them. And the most powerful way is reflection."

"Like summarizing what they said?"

"More than that. It's paraphrasing their meaning, their emotion, the thing beneath their words. Saying it back in a way that makes them feel genuinely understood." Sam drew two stick figures. Between them, arrows labeled "speaks" and "reflects."

"Someone shares something—a concern, an idea, a frustration. Before you respond with your own thoughts, you reflect back what you heard. Not word-for-word repetition, but the essence. Then you check: 'Is that right? Am I understanding you correctly?'"

"Seems simple."

"Simple but powerful. Most people go through life without feeling truly heard. When you reflect back accurately, something shifts. They feel understood. And that creates trust faster than almost anything else."

Sam turned to a new page. "Tell me something you're struggling with right now."

Jordan thought for a moment. "I'm worried that I've disrupted my team's confidence. They used to know exactly where they stood with me. Now everything's uncertain, and I wonder if I've made their work lives worse instead of better."

Sam counted to three, then spoke. "So you're concerned that in trying to develop them, you might have actually destabilized them. Like the medicine might be worse than the disease, at least in the short term. Is that right?"

Jordan felt something click. "Yes. Exactly that."

"See what happened? I didn't just repeat your words. I captured your worry and reflected it back in a way that showed I understood the deeper concern. And when I got it right, you felt heard."

"I did. It's weird how much that mattered."

"That's the echo effect. Your words came back transformed, clarified, validated. And now you trust that I actually get what you're experiencing." Sam closed his notebook. "This is especially powerful when someone's upset or resistant. Instead of defending yourself or solving their problem, you first show them you understand."

They resumed walking.

"Practice reflection with Taylor," Sam said. "When she says something important—especially if it's emotional or vulnerable—pause and reflect it back before moving to problem-solving."

"What if I get it wrong?"

"Then she'll correct you, and you'll try again. The attempt is what matters."

The opportunity came Friday afternoon. Taylor appeared in his doorway, but this time her expression wasn't angry. It was troubled.

"Do you have a few minutes?"

"Of course." Jordan closed his laptop.

Taylor sat down but didn't speak immediately.

"I've been thinking about our conversation," she finally said. "About growth and discomfort. And I realized something that's been bothering me."

Jordan waited.

"When you were the old Jordan—the one who told everyone what to do—I felt valuable. Like I had a clear role, and I was good at it. Now with all the questions and collaboration, I feel like I'm supposed to be someone I'm not. Like the skills that made me good before don't matter anymore."

Jordan's instinct was to reassure her. But he remembered Sam's instruction: reflect first.

He paused, really hearing what Taylor had said beneath the words.

"So it sounds like you're feeling a loss of identity," Jordan said slowly. "Like the person you were—the excellent executor—isn't valued in this new system. And you're not sure who you're supposed to be instead. Is that what you're experiencing?"

Taylor's eyes widened. "Yes. That's exactly it. I built my whole professional identity around being the person who could take complex directions and deliver results. And now that's not enough, but I don't know what is."

"And that's scary," Jordan added, "because you're starting from scratch in some ways. Learning a new role while feeling like the old one is being taken away."

"Yes!" Taylor leaned forward. "Everyone keeps saying this is growth, but it feels more like failure. Like I'm not good at the things that matter now."

Jordan felt the urge to jump in with solutions. Instead, he reflected again.

"So you're grieving, in a way. Grieving the loss of a role where you felt capable and confident. And you're being asked to embrace something new before you've had a chance to say goodbye to what you were good at."

Taylor's composure cracked slightly. "I hadn't thought of it as grieving, but yeah. That's what it feels like."

Jordan sat with the silence.

"Thank you for telling me that," Jordan said finally. "I didn't understand what this transition was costing you. I was so focused on the potential growth that I didn't acknowledge what you were losing."

"I know the execution role isn't enough long-term," Taylor said. "I know I need to develop other skills. But I guess I needed someone to acknowledge that it's hard. That I'm not just being resistant—I'm actually scared."

"You're scared that you won't be good at the new thing," Jordan reflected. "That you'll lose your identity as someone competent without gaining a new one to replace it."

"Exactly."

Jordan paused, feeling the weight of Taylor's trust. She was being vulnerable in a way she hadn't been before. Because he'd shown her he understood.

"Can I share what I see?"

Taylor nodded.

"I see someone who's been excellent at execution because you're organized, detail-oriented, and reliable. Those skills don't disappear in this new approach—they become the foundation for strategic thinking. The solution you came up with last week? That combined strategic thinking with your natural ability to see logistics. You didn't stop being an executor. You added a new layer to it."

Taylor absorbed this. "So I don't have to choose between old Taylor and new Taylor?"

"No. New Taylor includes everything old Taylor was good at, plus new capabilities you're developing. You're not replacing yourself. You're expanding yourself." Jordan leaned back. "But I get that it doesn't feel that way yet. Growth rarely feels like growth while it's happening."

"Like learning to walk," Taylor said quietly. "You have to fall a lot before you get steady."

"Exactly. And I should have told you that from the beginning."

Taylor smiled for the first time. "That's a terrible metaphor, but I appreciate it."

They talked for another twenty minutes. Jordan practiced reflection multiple times. Each time, Taylor's shoulders relaxed a little more.

"Thank you for this," Taylor said as she stood to leave. "For actually hearing me instead of just trying to fix me."

After Taylor left, Jordan sat at his desk feeling something shift. The conversation hadn't solved anything concrete. They hadn't created action items or plans.

But something more important had happened. Taylor felt understood. And that understanding had created a bridge between them that hadn't existed before.

Jordan texted Sam: "Used the echo effect with Taylor. You were right—it changed everything."

Sam's response: "When people feel heard, they stop defending and start connecting. Well done."

The following Thursday, Jordan arrived at the park feeling scattered. His phone had buzzed constantly all day—emails, questions, requests, calendar invitations.

Even now, walking toward Sam, Jordan's hand kept drifting to his phone.

"You look distracted," Sam observed.

"Sorry. Busy day." Jordan pulled out his phone to silence it, caught sight of new emails, and started to open them.

"Jordan."

He looked up.

"Put the phone away. All the way away. Not just silent—out of sight."

Jordan hesitated. "I'm expecting an update from—"

"It can wait thirty minutes. Put it away."

Jordan slipped the phone into his bag, feeling oddly naked. "Okay. Done."

"How does that feel?"

"Uncomfortable. Like I'm missing something important."

"Even though we scheduled this meeting a week ago? Even though everyone knows you're unavailable right now?"

Jordan recognized where this was heading. "I know it's irrational. But yes."

Sam nodded. "Tell me about yesterday. Walk me through it."

"Got to the office around seven-thirty. Checked emails while drinking coffee. Team meeting at nine. Back-to-back one-on-ones from ten to noon. Working lunch reviewing the Henderson proposal. Two hours of project work. Client call at three. Wrapped up emails until six-thirty."

"And during the team meeting—were you fully present?"

Jordan started to say yes, then stopped. "I was there physically. But I was also thinking about the one-on-ones coming up. And I checked my phone twice when I thought people weren't watching."

"During the one-on-ones?"

"I was present for those. Mostly. Though I was definitely aware of time because they were scheduled so tightly."

"Project work?"

"Interrupted five times. So I'd focus for ten minutes, get pulled away, then try to refocus."

Sam pulled out his notebook. "So in an eleven-hour workday, how many hours were you actually present? Fully engaged with what was happening in that moment?"

Jordan thought honestly. "Maybe two hours. The one-on-ones and part of the project work."

"Which means for nine hours, you were physically somewhere but mentally somewhere else. Planning the next thing, worrying about what you missed." Sam wrote numbers. "What if I told you that those two hours of presence were worth more than the nine hours of distracted productivity?"

"I'd say that's impossible. I got things done during those nine hours."

"Did you? Or did you just stay busy?" Sam's tone was gentle but challenging. "When you're in a meeting thinking about the next meeting, are you really in the meeting? When you're with one person while checking your phone, are you really with them?"

Jordan felt defensive. "I'm managing a team and multiple projects. I have to stay on top of things."

"Do you? Or have you convinced yourself that constant availability equals productivity?" Sam leaned back. "You've learned to pause, to ask questions, to listen for potential, to reflect back what you hear. These are beautiful skills. But they only work if you're actually present when you use them."

A mother pushed a stroller past them. The fountain created its background music.

"I don't understand how to be more present," Jordan admitted. "I'm showing up, I'm participating."

"There's the difference between attendance and presence. Attendance is being physically there. Presence is being mentally and emotionally there. No part of you thinking about the past or future. All of you engaged with what's happening right now."

Sam turned to face Jordan directly. "When's the last time you were in a conversation and weren't planning your response while the other person was talking?"

Jordan realized he couldn't remember.

"When's the last time you were in a meeting and weren't thinking about your next meeting?"

No answer came.

"When's the last time someone was talking to you and you noticed the expression in their eyes, the tone of their voice—not as a technique, but because you were so fully there that you couldn't help but notice?"

Jordan felt something uncomfortable settling in his chest. "You're saying I'm never really present."

"I'm saying you've trained yourself to be everywhere except where you are. And that training is killing your effectiveness as a leader."

The words stung because they were true.

"Here's what you need to understand," Sam continued. "The highest form of productivity isn't getting more done. It's being fully engaged with what you're doing. Because when you're present— truly present—the quality of everything improves. Your questions get sharper. Your listening gets deeper. Your decisions get wiser. Your relationships get stronger."

"But I have responsibilities. Things that need my attention."

"And they'll get your best attention when you give them your full attention, one at a time, instead of your partial attention to everything simultaneously."

Sam gestured to the path. "You can walk this path while checking your phone, planning your next meeting, thinking about tomorrow. You'll get from point A to point B. But you'll miss the walk entirely. Or you can walk it fully present—feeling your feet on the ground, noticing the trees, breathing the air. You still get from A to B, but the experience is completely different. And you arrive more centered, more clear, more ready for what comes next."

"What would it look like to be fully present?"

"Start with one-on-ones. When someone comes to your office, you close your laptop. You silence your phone and put it away. You clear your mind of whatever you were working on. And for those twenty or thirty minutes, that person is the only thing that exists in your world."

"That sounds inefficient."

"Your attention—your full, undivided attention—is so rare that when someone receives it, they remember. They feel valued in a way that no amount of partial attention can create."

Sam stood. "Here's your assignment. Two weeks of practicing presence. In meetings, in one-on-ones, even in casual conversations—be fully there. Notice when your mind wanders. Notice when you're physically present but mentally absent. And gently bring yourself back."

"That's it? Just notice?"

"Noticing is everything. You can't change what you don't see."

Jordan felt overwhelmed. "I don't know if I can do this."

"Tell me something. When you think about the best boss you ever had, what do you remember?"

Jordan thought back. A manager named Patricia who'd helped him navigate his first major client crisis. "She made me feel like I was the most important thing in the world when we talked. Like nothing else mattered but helping me figure out the problem."

"Was she actually ignoring everything else?"

"No, she was probably just as busy as I am now. But in those moments with me, it felt like I was all that existed."

"That's presence. That's what you remember, years later. Not her productivity or her multitasking ability. The quality of her attention." Sam shouldered his bag. "Give your team that gift. Two weeks. See what happens."

Jordan tried. He really tried.

Monday morning, Devon came with a question. Jordan closed his laptop. Put his phone in a drawer. Made eye contact.

Devon explained the challenge. Jordan listened, feeling his mind drift to the team meeting in twenty minutes. He noticed the drift and pulled his attention back. Devon's words. Devon's concern. Just this moment.

"What options are you considering?"

They worked through it. When Jordan's mind wandered—four times in ten minutes—he noticed it and returned his focus.

The conversation lasted twelve minutes. At the end, Devon said, "Thanks for really listening. That helped a lot."

Tuesday, Jordan practiced presence in the team meeting. No checking his phone. No thinking about what came next.

He lasted about fifteen minutes before his mind started cataloging tasks. He noticed, brought himself back. Five minutes later, same thing. Notice, return. Over and over.

It was exhausting.

Wednesday, Jordan had three back-to-back one-on-ones. Normally he'd prep for each one during the previous one. This time, he committed to being fully present.

The first one with Marcus ran ten minutes over because Jordan wasn't watching the clock. The second with Jamal felt deeper, more connected. The third with Kevin revealed insights Jordan would have missed.

His schedule was now behind by fifteen minutes. His instinct screamed inefficiency.

But all three people had left his office looking energized, heard, valued.

The second week, something shifted.

Jordan stopped fighting the presence and started leaning into it. Meetings still ran long sometimes, but the decisions made were better. One-on-one's felt less like checking boxes and more like genuine development conversations.

Friday afternoon, Taylor stopped by his office.

"You seem different this week," she said.

"Different how?"

"More... here. Less like you're already thinking about the next thing." She smiled. "I like it."

After she left, Jordan sat at his desk as the afternoon sun slanted through his window. He'd accomplished less this week in terms of tasks checked off. But he'd accomplished more in terms of relationships deepened, thinking sharpened, team development advanced.

Maybe Sam was right.

Maybe presence was the highest form of productivity after all.

CHAPTER 14: THE CRISIS

The email arrived at 7:42 AM on a Tuesday, three weeks into Jordan's practice of presence.

Subject: URGENT - Morrison Account Issue

Jordan opened it, coffee halfway to his lips.

"Jordan - Morrison's CFO just informed us they're terminating the contract effective immediately. Citing performance issues and missed deliverables on the Q1 integration project. This is a $200K annual account and a major reference client. I need you in my office at 9 AM with a plan to fix this. - David Chen"

Jordan's stomach dropped. Morrison was their third-largest account. Losing them would crater his team's numbers for the year. And worse—he had no idea what performance issues or missed deliverables David was referring to. The Morrison account had been humming along smoothly as far as Jordan knew.

He immediately pulled up the project files. The Q1 integration had been Marcus's responsibility. Jordan scanned through status reports from the past two months. All green. On track. No issues flagged.

How had this happened?

Jordan's phone buzzed. A text from Marcus: "Just saw the Morrison email you forwarded from David. Can we talk before the 9am meeting?"

"My office, 8am," Jordan replied.

The hour between now and then felt like standing on the edge of a cliff. Jordan's mind raced through options. Call Morrison's CFO directly and try to salvage it. Put together a recovery plan. Offer a discount. Assign someone else to the account.

No—first he needed to understand what actually went wrong.

Marcus appeared at 8 AM looking pale.

"Tell me what happened," Jordan said, gesturing for Marcus to close the door and sit.

"I don't fully know. I got a voicemail from Morrison's project manager yesterday afternoon saying they needed to talk urgently. I called back three times but couldn't reach her. Then this morning, the termination email." Marcus pulled up his laptop. "According to our records, we delivered everything on time. But apparently Morrison's team is saying we missed two critical milestones and didn't communicate about delays."

"Did we miss them?"

"Not according to our project plan. But..." Marcus hesitated. "There might have been a disconnect between our understanding of the milestones and theirs. Early in the project, their PM mentioned some additional checkpoints they wanted. I noted them, but I didn't formally add them to the statement of work because they seemed redundant with what we were already doing."

Jordan felt the familiar surge of frustration. Why hadn't Marcus escalated this? Why hadn't he confirmed the scope in writing?

But underneath the frustration, Jordan recognized his own role. Had he created an environment where Marcus felt comfortable raising scope questions? Or had Jordan been so focused on efficiency that Marcus had learned to make judgment calls without bothering his manager?

"Okay," Jordan said, pushing down the urge to criticize. "What else do I need to know before this meeting with David?"

"Morrison's team is upset. The project manager sent an email last week—I didn't see it until this morning because it went to an old distribution list—saying they felt blindsided by our approach and that communication had broken down. She tried to raise concerns in three separate calls, but apparently whoever she talked to didn't understand the severity."

Jordan closed his eyes briefly. This was worse than a simple missed deliverable. This was a relationship breakdown. A failure of communication and trust.

"Who did she talk to?" Jordan asked.

"I don't know. The email didn't specify."

Jordan looked at the clock. 8:10 AM. Fifty minutes until he had to walk into David's office with a plan.

Old Jordan would have spent those Fifty minutes crafting the plan alone. Identifying the failures, designing the recovery strategy, preparing talking points. He would have walked into David's office with answers.

But old Jordan's approach had created this situation—a team that didn't communicate problems up, that made judgment calls in isolation, that let relationships deteriorate without escalating.

New Jordan needed to do this differently.

"Get the team together," Jordan said. "Conference Room B, right now. Everyone."

"Everyone? We have Forty-eight minutes.", glancing at his watch.

"Then we have Forty-eight minutes. Go."

Marcus sent the urgent message while Jordan grabbed his laptop. By 8:15, all five team members were assembled, looking confused and anxious.

"You've all seen the Morrison email," Jordan said. "We have a major client threatening to walk, senior leadership demanding answers, and eight minutes before I have to present a solution. Here's what I know." He quickly summarized what Marcus had shared. "Here's what I don't know—how this happened, what we missed, and how to fix it."

He paused, feeling his heart racing. Every instinct screamed at him to take control, to direct, to solve. To protect his team by owning the failure himself and presenting a plan to David.

Instead, he said, "I need your best", then the hardest words he'd spoken as a manager:

"What do we do?"

Silence fell over the room. His team looked at each other, then back at Jordan.

The old pattern would have been for Jordan to wait maybe three seconds, then jump in with his solution. Instead, he started counting in his head.

One. Two. Three.

The silence felt excruciating. He could see David's office in his mind, could imagine the disappointment on his boss's face when Jordan showed up with nothing.

Four. Five. Six.

Taylor spoke first. "We need to understand what Morrison's team actually thinks went wrong before we try to fix it. Maybe we can call them right now?"

"Good," Jordan said. "What else?"

Seven. Eight.

"We need to own the communication breakdown," Jamal said. "Not make excuses about distribution lists or scope documents. Just acknowledge we failed to stay connected with their needs."

Nine. Ten.

"What about a recovery plan?" Kevin asked. "Even if we don't know all the details yet, we could propose immediate actions. Like assigning a dedicated liaison, daily check-ins for the next two weeks, a formal review of all deliverables against their expectations."

Jordan wrote rapidly, capturing every idea. His instinct was to shape them, to refine them, to add his own improvements. He bit his tongue and kept writing.

"The relationship is broken," Devon added. "Fixing the project won't matter if they don't trust us. We need to rebuild trust first, then worry about deliverables."

"How do we rebuild trust in—" Jordan glanced at the clock, "—thirty minutes?"

"We can't," Marcus said quietly. "But we can start by being completely transparent about what happened. No spin, no corporate language. Just honesty about where we failed and what we're going to do differently."

Taylor pulled out her phone. "I'm calling Morrison's project manager right now. If she answers, we put her on speaker and we all listen to what she has to say. Even if it's painful."

Jordan felt a flash of panic. An unplanned, unscripted conversation with an angry client while his entire team listened? That was messy, risky, potentially disastrous.

It was also exactly what the situation needed.

"Do it," Jordan said.

Taylor dialed. The phone rang once, twice, three times. Jordan prepared himself for voicemail.

"Hello?" A woman's voice, wary.

"Hi Jennifer, this is Taylor from Jordan Vale's team. I'm here with Jordan and the entire Morrison account team. We just got word about the contract termination, and we want to understand what happened. Can you talk for a few minutes?"

"I've been trying to talk for three weeks," Jennifer said, her frustration clear. "Nobody seemed to be listening."

"You're right," Jordan said, "and I apologize. We're listening now. Can you tell us what went wrong from your perspective?"

What followed was five minutes of painful honesty. Jennifer described how the integration project had veered from Morrison's expectations in the first month. How she'd tried to course-correct through calls and emails that went unanswered or received generic responses. How the deliverables Morrison received didn't match what their leadership had been told to expect. How she'd felt increasingly ignored and frustrated.

"I tried to tell your team we needed daily syncs during the critical phase," Jennifer said. "Instead, I got weekly status emails that didn't address our actual concerns. I tried to explain our CFO needed visibility into specific metrics. Instead, I got standard reports. It felt like you were delivering what was convenient for you, not what we needed."

Jordan's team sat in stunned silence. Marcus looked stricken. Taylor was taking notes rapidly.

"Jennifer," Jordan said, "thank you for being direct. You deserved better communication from us, and you didn't get it. That's on me and my team. What would it take for you to give us a chance to make this right?"

A pause. "Honestly? I don't know if my CFO will even consider it at this point. He's already talking to your competitors."

"What if we could show you—today—that we understand what broke down and we have a concrete plan to prevent it from happening again? Not promises, but actual structural changes to how we work with you."

Another pause. "I'd be willing to listen. But Jordan, it can't just be words. We need to see real change."

"Understood. Can we call you back in by 11:00?"

"By 11:00. Okay."

The call ended. Jordan looked at the clock. 8:59. David's meeting was now.

"Here's what we're going to do," Jordan said. "I'm going to ask David for one hour. I'm going to tell him we're working on a real solution, not a band-aid, and we need time to do it right. You all are going to stay here and build that solution."

"What do you want us to focus on?" Marcus asked.

Jordan almost answered. Almost laid out the framework, the priorities, the structure. Instead, he said, "What do you think you should focus on?"

Kevin spoke up. "Three things. First, immediate actions to show Morrison we're serious—probably the dedicated liaison and daily syncs Jennifer mentioned. Second, structural changes to how we manage accounts to prevent this from happening in the future. Third, a relationship repair plan specific to Jennifer and her team, because they're the ones we hurt."

"One hour," Taylor said. "We can draft all three and have something concrete to present to David, then Jennifer."

Jordan stood. "I'm trusting you to solve this. I'll be back once I talk to David. Make it work."

He walked to David's office, his heart pounding but his mind clear. For the first time in his career, he was walking into a crisis meeting without a complete plan.

But he had something better. He had a team that was thinking, engaged, and solving—not waiting for him to rescue them.

David looked up as Jordan entered. "Close the door. What's the plan?"

"The plan is being built right now by my team," Jordan said. "Can we have an hour to come back with something real?"

David frowned. "You don't have a plan ready?"

"I have the beginning of one. But I learned something this morning—the reason we're in this crisis is that I've been solving problems instead of developing my team's ability to solve them. Morrison fell through the cracks because Marcus was making decisions in isolation instead of collaborating. And he was doing that because I trained him to."

Jordan took a breath. "So instead of me crafting a recovery plan alone, my entire team is working on it together right now. We have already called the Project Manager, Jennifer, to better understand what really broke down, and building a solution that addresses root causes, not just symptoms and asked if we could call her by 11:00l. Give me an hour to bring you something that will actually work long term."

David studied him for a long moment. "One hour. But Jordan, this account matters. If your new leadership approach can't handle a crisis, we need to know that now."

"Understood."

Jordan walked back to Conference Room B. Through the glass wall, he could see his team in animated discussion. Taylor was on the whiteboard. Kevin was typing rapidly. Marcus was on a call—probably researching what competitors were offering Morrison.

They were solving it.

Not waiting for Jordan to tell them how.

Actually solving it.

He opened the door. Five faces looked up.

"You've got forty-five minutes," Jordan said. "Then we present to David together. What do you need from me?"

"Just trust us," Devon said.

Jordan smiled. "I do."

He sat down and watched his team work. Occasionally they asked him questions—about budget authority, about what David would need to see, about Morrison's history. But they didn't ask him to solve.

They were doing that themselves.

At 10:00, they walked into David's office together. Taylor presented the immediate actions. Kevin outlined the structural changes. Marcus delivered the relationship repair plan, owning his mistakes with painful honesty.

At 10:30, they called Jennifer back and presented the same plan. Her skepticism was palpable, but so was her cautious willingness to try.

"We'll give you two weeks," Jennifer said. "Daily syncs starting tomorrow. If we see real change, we'll reconsider the termination."

After the call ended, Jordan's team erupted in relieved celebration. They'd pulled it off. Stopped the crisis. Created a path forward.

David pulled Jordan aside. "That was impressive. Not the plan itself—though it's solid—but the way your team owned it. I've never seen them operate like that."

"Neither have I," Jordan admitted. "But I'm learning that's because I never let them."

Walking back to his office, Jordan felt something shift fundamentally. The crisis hadn't been solved by his expertise or his quick thinking. It had been solved by a team that he'd finally empowered to actually think.

The old Jordan would have saved the day alone.

The new Jordan had let his team save it together.

And their solution was better than anything he would have created on his own.

CHAPTER 15: THE TRUST COMPOUND

Six weeks after the Morrison crisis, Jordan sat in his office reviewing the latest engagement survey results. The quarterly data had just come through, and he'd been almost afraid to open it.

Now, staring at the screen, he read the number three times to make sure he wasn't misreading it.

Team engagement score: 87 out of 100.

Up from 72 last quarter. A fifteen-point jump. The kind of increase that typically took years, not months.

Jordan scrolled through the comments.

"Jordan has completely transformed how he leads. I feel heard and valued."

"Our team meetings are actual discussions now, not just Jordan telling us what to do."

"I'm learning and growing more than I have in years."

"Jordan trusts us to think, and that makes me want to bring my best thinking."

He sat back in his chair, letting it sink in. Three months ago, he'd been losing his best employee and watching his team languish in mediocrity. Now they were approaching the performance levels of Alex's and Vanessa's teams.

Not because Jordan had become smarter or worked harder.

Because he'd learned to get out of their way.

A knock on his doorframe interrupted his thoughts. Taylor stood there with Kevin, both holding laptops.

"Got a minute?" Taylor asked. "We have an idea we want to run by you."

"Of course, come in."

They settled into the chairs across from his desk. Jordan noticed immediately that Taylor's demeanor had changed from even a few weeks ago. She sat forward, energized rather than guarded.

"Kevin and I were talking about the Morrison recovery," Taylor began. "The daily syncs and dedicated liaison approach is working really well. Jennifer even emailed yesterday saying they're seeing the best communication they've had with us in two years."

"That's great to hear," Jordan said.

"Right, but here's the thing—we're only doing that intensive approach with Morrison because they almost left. What if we're being reactive when we should be proactive?" Taylor opened her laptop. "Kevin and I mapped out all our major accounts. Eight of them show similar warning signs that Morrison had three months ago. Not critical yet, but trending toward communication breakdowns."

Kevin jumped in. "We're proposing a tiered account management system. Top accounts get weekly syncs and a dedicated liaison. Mid-tier accounts get bi-weekly check-ins with structured feedback loops. We'd catch problems before they become crises."

Jordan's first instinct was to evaluate the idea, to poke holes in it, to add his own improvements. Instead, he paused and really looked at what they'd presented.

The analysis was thorough. They'd identified not just the at-risk accounts but the specific indicators they were tracking. The proposed solution was detailed, with resource requirements, implementation timeline, and success metrics already mapped out.

This wasn't a half-baked idea brought to him for completion. This was a complete strategy brought to him for validation.

"Walk me through how you'd resource this," Jordan said. "We don't have unlimited capacity."

Taylor flipped to another slide. "We reallocated based on account value and risk. Some low-value accounts that currently get weekly check-ins would move to monthly. That frees up time for the high-value, at-risk accounts to get more attention. Net result is the same total hours, just distributed more strategically."

"What about the accounts we're reducing attention to? Risk of losing them?"

"We thought about that," Kevin said. "Most of them are stable, long-term relationships with low complexity. They don't need weekly check-ins—we've just been doing it out of habit. We'd still be proactive, but due to the size of their companies, they do not need as much allocation."

Jordan felt something close to pride. Not in himself, but in watching these two think through problems with sophistication he hadn't seen from them before.

"Have you talked to Marcus and the others about this?" Jordan asked.

"Not yet," Taylor said. "We wanted your input first. But if you think it's worth pursuing, we'd like to present it to the full team and get their feedback before finalizing."

"I think it's worth pursuing. When do you want to present to the team?"

"Friday's meeting?" Kevin suggested.

"Perfect. You two take the lead on that agenda item. I'll make sure everyone's seen your analysis beforehand so we can have a productive discussion."

After they left, Jordan sat with what had just happened. Taylor and Kevin had identified a problem, analyzed it thoroughly, developed a solution, and brought it to him ready for implementation. Three months ago, they would have waited for Jordan to notice the problem and tell them how to fix it.

The shift was remarkable.

Wednesday afternoon, Marcus stopped by Jordan's office.

"Henderson just agreed to extend their contract for three years," Marcus said, grinning. "And they want to expand scope to include the innovation framework I originally proposed."

Jordan remembered that first team meeting, back in March. Marcus suggesting they lead with innovation, Jordan redirecting him toward cost savings instead.

"Tell me about the conversation," Jordan said.

"I used the exact pitch I'd wanted to use three months ago. Led with their CEO's concerns about disruption, positioned us as innovation partners, showed how our approach would keep them ahead of market changes. They loved it." Marcus sat down without being invited—another small change Jordan noticed. "The funny thing is, your cost-savings approach got us the initial renewal. But the innovation angle is what got us the expansion. Both were needed."

"So your instinct was right back in March."

"Maybe. Or maybe the timing is right now in a way it wasn't then." Marcus paused. "But I appreciate that you've been letting me run with these ideas instead of redirecting me. It's made a huge difference in how I approach client relationships."

After Marcus left, Jordan checked his calendar. Team meeting Friday, then his standing Thursday session with Sam. He pulled out his notebook and started writing notes about the past few weeks.

Small moments that had compounded into something larger:

- Devon leading the client appreciation event planning, which had been a massive success. Clients raved about the interactive format. Three had already signed contract extensions.

- Kevin's portal integration project finishing two weeks early and under budget, his systems thinking proving invaluable.

- Taylor not just accepting the collaborative approach but championing it, pulling Kevin into the account management analysis without Jordan's prompting.

- Jamal bringing a complete marketing strategy for Q3 that Jordan had approved with minimal changes because it was genuinely excellent.

- The team's Slack channel filling with ideas, questions, and collaborative problem-solving that happened without Jordan's involvement.

None of these were dramatic transformations. Each was a small shift, an incremental improvement, a quiet moment of growth.

But together, they'd created something Jordan hadn't fully appreciated until now: a team that functioned as a team, not as a collection of individuals waiting for his direction.

Thursday afternoon at the park, Jordan shared the engagement scores with Sam.

"Eighty-seven," Sam repeated. "That's exceptional growth. How do you feel about it?"

"Honestly? Surprised it happened this fast. And a little worried it's not sustainable."

"Why worried?"

"Because it still feels new. Fragile. Like if I have one bad week and slip back into old habits, everything could unravel."

Sam smiled. "That's reasonable caution. But let me offer a different perspective. What you're seeing now isn't fragile—it's compound interest on trust."

He pulled out his notebook and drew a simple graph. "Trust doesn't grow linearly. It compounds. Every time you listen instead of solve, you make a deposit. Every time you create space instead of filling it, another deposit. and every time you reflect back instead of jumping to solutions, yet another deposit."

Sam drew the line curving upward. "At first, the returns are small. You make deposits for weeks and barely see results. But once you hit critical mass, the growth accelerates. Your team starts trusting not just that you'll listen this time, but that this is genuinely who you are now. And that unlocking creates exponential growth."

"So the six weeks of slow progress..."

"Were building the foundation. Now you're seeing the compound returns." Sam tapped the upward curve. "And here's the beautiful part—it gets easier from here, not harder. Because your team is doing the work of developing themselves and each other. You're not the sole source of growth anymore."

Jordan thought about Taylor and Kevin's initiative, about Marcus's confidence, about Devon's leadership on the client event.

"They're teaching each other," Jordan said slowly.

"Exactly. You created the conditions. They're creating the culture. That's when you know the transformation is real—when it's no longer dependent on you sustaining it every single day."

They walked along the riverside path. The late June heat had settled over the city, but under the trees, a breeze made it pleasant.

"Can I tell you what I'm most proud of?" Jordan asked.

"Please."

"It's not the engagement scores, or the client wins or even the fact that my team is performing better. It's that I actually enjoy work now in a way I didn't before." Jordan kicked a loose stone on the path. "I used to go home exhausted from carrying everything. Now I go home energized because I'm watching people grow. The work feels lighter even though we're accomplishing more."

"That's the paradox of delegation," Sam said. "When you hold everything yourself, the load is heavy. When you distribute it, everyone carries less and accomplishes more. You discovered what every great leader eventually learns—your job isn't to be Atlas holding up the world. It's to build a team strong enough that the world holds itself up."

They reached their usual bench and sat. The fountain sparkled in the afternoon sun.

"What's next?" Jordan asked. "I feel like I'm finally getting this, but I don't want to get complacent."

"Next you become the mentor," Sam said. "You've received this gift of transformation. Now you pass it on. Someone else is where you were three months ago—capable manager, decent results, no idea they're limiting their team. You help them see what you couldn't see. You give them what Alex gave you."

Jordan thought about the young manager Chris who'd approached him after that leadership workshop months ago, asking for advice. Jordan had been too caught up in his own struggles to follow up.

Maybe it was time to change that.

"I can do that," Jordan said.

"I know you can. Because you've lived it. And people trust transformation stories from those who've actually transformed, not from those who just talk about it." Sam stood to leave. "Same time next week?"

"Actually," Jordan said, "I'm wondering if we should shift to monthly instead of weekly. Not because I don't value our conversations, but because I think I need to practice running on my own for a while. Make sure I can sustain this without weekly guidance."

Sam's smile was knowing. "That's exactly the right instinct. Monthly it is. Call me if you hit any walls, but I suspect you won't. You've got this now."

After Sam left, Jordan sat on the bench a while longer, watching the water, watching people pass by in their daily rhythms.

Three months ago, he'd sat in this park desperate for answers, convinced he was failing as a leader.

Now he understood that the answers had never been the point.

The questions were.

The listening was.

The space he created was.

And the trust that compounded from all those small moments when he chose to develop instead of direct, to ask instead of answer, to listen instead of lead with certainty.

His phone buzzed. A message from Taylor: "Kevin and I finished the presentation for Friday. Want us to send it to you for review or just share it with the team directly?"

Jordan typed back: "Share it with the team. I trust your judgment."

Three words that would have been impossible to write three months ago.

Three words that now felt completely natural.

I trust your judgment.

The foundation of everything he'd learned.

The compound interest paying dividends every single day.

CHAPTER 16: THE STUDENT BECOMES THE TEACHER

The email from Alex arrived on a Tuesday morning in mid-July.

"Hey Jordan - I'm running a leadership development workshop next month for mid-level managers. Would you be willing to share your story? 20 minutes on your transformation over the past few months. I think people would benefit from hearing how you shifted your approach. Let me know! - Alex"

Jordan stared at the message, feeling equal parts flattered and terrified.

Share his story? In front of other managers? Talk about his failures, his struggles, the painful exit interview with Sofia that had started everything?

His finger hovered over the reply button. The old Jordan would have declined politely, citing a busy schedule or lack of public speaking experience. Sharing vulnerability wasn't something managers did. Leaders were supposed to project confidence, competence, and certainty.

But that was old thinking.

Jordan typed: "I'd be honored. When and where?"

Alex's response came immediately: "August 12th, 2pm. Conference Center downtown. You're a lifesaver. This is going to be great."

The next three weeks, Jordan couldn't stop thinking about what to say. He started and deleted four different presentations. Each attempt felt too polished, too sanitized, like he was packaging his transformation into neat bullet points that missed the messy reality.

Finally, he called Sam.

"I'm supposed to speak at this workshop," Jordan explained. "But every time I try to prepare remarks, they sound fake. Like I'm pretending the journey was cleaner than it actually was."

"So don't pretend," Sam said simply. "Tell the truth. The real story, not the highlight reel."

"People don't want to hear about all my failures."

"People desperately want to hear about failures. Success stories are a dime a dozen. But honest accounts of struggling, failing, and growing? Those are rare. Those are valuable." Sam paused. "What are you afraid of?"

Jordan thought about it. "That I'll look incompetent. That other managers will think I was a terrible leader who barely figured it out."

"And what if they think that?"

"Then..." Jordan trailed off. "Then they'd be right. I was barely figuring it out. I still am some days."

"Exactly. And that honesty is what will help them. Because most of them are also barely figuring it out, but they think they're the only ones. You give them permission to be human."

The conversation shifted something for Jordan. He stopped trying to craft a polished presentation and instead just wrote what had actually happened. The spreadsheet full of yellow cells. Sofia's devastating exit interview. The failed attempts to change. The gradual, uncomfortable progress. The moments of breakthrough.

No corporate jargon. No leadership frameworks dressed up in buzzwords. Just the truth.

August 12th arrived hot and humid. The conference center's air conditioning worked overtime against the summer heat. Jordan arrived thirty minutes early, dressed in business casual, carrying nothing but a single notecard with three words written on it: "Be honest. Be helpful."

The room filled with about forty managers, most around Jordan's age or younger. Alex introduced the session, talking about the importance of evolving leadership approaches and learning from each other's experiences.

Then she introduced Jordan.

"Jordan Vale leads a team in our client services division. Three months ago, his team was performing adequately but not exceptionally. Today, they're one of our top-performing teams with engagement scores that rival the best in the company. He's going to share how that transformation happened. Jordan?"

He stood and walked to the front of the room. Forty faces looked at him expectantly.

Jordan took a breath.

"Three months ago, I lost my best employee," he began. "She quit and went to a competitor. In her exit interview, she told me I never actually heard her ideas. That I made my whole team feel like highly paid assistants instead of valued contributors. And she was absolutely right."

He saw a few people shift in their seats. This wasn't the typical leadership success story opening.

"I thought I was a good manager. My teams delivered results. Projects got done. I worked hard, stayed on top of details, always had answers. But what I didn't realize was that having all the answers was preventing my team from developing the ability to find their own answers."

Jordan walked through the story. The performance data showing him stuck in mediocrity while peers like Alex excelled. Watching Alex's team meeting and seeing a completely different dynamic. His own failed attempts to change. The mentorship with Sam.

"The first assignment my mentor gave me was to run one meeting without offering solutions. Just ask questions and create space. I lasted about thirty seconds before jumping in with my own ideas." A few people laughed, recognizing themselves. "And I felt like a complete failure. Because I'd built my entire identity as a manager around being the person with answers."

He described the discomfort of pausing before responding. The anxiety of creating silence. The resistance from team members who wanted him to just tell them what to do. The slow, frustrating process of learning to listen instead of solve.

"About six weeks in, we had a major crisis. Big client threatening to leave, senior leadership demanding answers. Every instinct told me to take control, to solve it myself, to be the hero." Jordan paused. "Instead, I asked my team: 'I need your best thinking. What do we do?' Then I forced myself to stay quiet and let them figure it out."

131

He described how terrifying those moments had felt. And how his team had come up with a solution better than anything he would have created alone.

"Here's what I learned. The less I talked, the more influence I actually had. My silence gave my team permission to think, to grow, to own their work in ways they never could when I was solving everything for them."

Jordan looked around the room. People were leaning forward, engaged. Some were taking notes. A few nodded in recognition.

"I'm not standing here as someone who's perfected this. I still catch myself jumping in too quickly. I still feel the urge to solve instead of coach. But my team's engagement scores went from 72 to 87 in three months. Not because I got smarter or worked harder. Because I finally got out of their way."

He wrapped up with the most important lesson. "If you take nothing else from this, take this: your job as a leader isn't to have the best answers. It's to unlock your team's ability to find answers. Those are completely different jobs. And making that shift is uncomfortable, messy, and one of the most valuable things you'll ever do."

The room was silent for a moment after he finished. Then someone started clapping. Others joined. Not polite applause but genuine appreciation.

Alex stood. "Thank you, Jordan. That was incredibly honest and helpful. We have time for a few questions."

Hands shot up around the room. For the next twenty minutes, Jordan fielded questions about specific techniques, about handling resistance, about staying consistent when the old way felt easier.

He answered as honestly as he could. Sometimes with "I don't know, I'm still figuring that out." Sometimes with specific examples from his team. But, always with the underlying message: this is hard, it's worth it, and you don't have to be perfect.

When the session ended, people clustered around him. Several shared their own struggles with similar challenges. A few asked for his email to continue the conversation.

As the crowd thinned, Jordan noticed a young man hanging back, waiting. When everyone else had left, he approached.

"Jordan? I'm Chris Patterson. I manage a team in operations." He looked nervous. "Everything you described—the having all the answers, the team waiting for direction, the feeling like you're helping when you're actually limiting them—that's exactly where I am right now."

Jordan recognized the look on Chris's face. The same desperate confusion he'd felt in Sofia's exit interview. The realization that something fundamental was wrong but not knowing how to fix it.

"I've been managing for about eighteen months," Chris continued. "My reviews are good, my team delivers, but I can tell something's off. They don't seem engaged. They don't bring me ideas, just problems. And I'm exhausted from carrying everything." He paused. "I'm where you were three months ago. Can we talk? Like, really talk? I need help."

Jordan felt something click into place. This was what Sam had meant about becoming the mentor. About passing on the gift of transformation.

"Yes," Jordan said. "Absolutely we can talk. Do you have time for coffee right now?"

Relief flooded Chris's face. "Really? Yes, definitely."

They walked to a café two blocks from the conference center. Jordan ordered his usual cappuccino, Chris got an iced coffee. They found a quiet table in the corner.

"Tell me what's happening with your team," Jordan said.

Chris poured out his story. Eight people reporting to him, all competent, all delivering acceptable work. But turnover was higher than he'd like. Engagement scores were mediocre. And Chris felt like he was working seventy-hour weeks while his team worked forty.

"I thought that was just the job of a manager," Chris said. "Work harder than everyone else, have all the answers, solve all the problems. But I'm burning out, and I don't think my team is growing."

Jordan heard his own voice from a few months ago. The same assumptions, the same exhaustion, the same sense that something was wrong without knowing what.

"What if I told you," Jordan said, "that your job isn't to work harder than everyone else or have all the answers? What if your job is to develop your team's ability to work hard and find their own answers?"

Chris looked skeptical. "But if I'm not solving problems, what am I doing?"

"Creating the conditions where others can solve problems. Asking questions instead of providing answers. Building capability instead of demonstrating your own." Jordan paused, using Sam's technique. "How does that land for you?"

"It sounds great in theory. But in practice, if I don't solve things, they don't get solved."

"Have you actually tested that? Or have you trained your team to wait for you to solve things because that's what you've always done?"

Chris sat with that question. "I guess I haven't really tested it. I just assume they need me to."

Jordan spent the next hour sharing what he'd learned. Not as a polished framework, but as raw experience. The discomfort of changing. The resistance from team members. The small wins that eventually compounded into transformation.

"Here's what I'd suggest," Jordan said. "Start with one person on your team. Someone you trust. Have a conversation where you're fully present—phone away, laptop closed, nothing else on your mind. Ask them what they think about a challenge they're facing. Then count to five before responding. Just listen and be curious."

"That's it?" Chris asked.

"That's the start. See what happens when you create space instead of filling it. See what your team member does with that space." Jordan pulled out a business card and wrote his cell number on the back. "Try it this week. Then call me and tell me how it went. I'll help you figure out next steps."

Chris took the card like it was something precious. "Thank you. Seriously. I didn't know who else to ask."

"I know exactly how that feels," Jordan said. "Someone helped me when I needed it. Now I'm helping you. Someday you'll help someone else. That's how this works."

After Chris left, Jordan sat at the café table a bit longer. The afternoon sun streamed through the windows. The barista called out drink orders. Normal life continuing while something significant had just happened.

He'd become the mentor.

The student who'd been desperate for guidance three months ago was now offering that guidance to someone else.

Jordan pulled out his phone and texted Sam: "Just had coffee with a young manager who's exactly where I was in March. Feels full circle."

Sam's response came quickly: "That's when you know the transformation is complete—when you can help others transform. Proud of you."

Jordan pocketed his phone and headed back to the office. He had a team meeting at four, and Taylor wanted to discuss expanding the account management system to all clients, not just the at-risk ones.

His team didn't need him to have all the answers anymore.

And now Jordan was learning he didn't need to have them either.

He just needed to help others discover theirs.

"Leadership is unlocking people's potential to become better."

— Bill Bradley

CHAPTER 17: THE QUIET RIPPLE

August had given way to September. The air carried the first hints of fall, though the trees hadn't quite started turning yet. Jordan walked the familiar riverside path to meet Sam, noticing how different he felt from the first time he'd made this walk a few months ago.

Back then, he'd been desperate, drowning, convinced he was failing at something fundamental he couldn't name.

Now he felt steady. Not perfect. Not finished. But grounded in a way he'd never experienced as a leader.

Sam was waiting at their usual bench, two coffees already purchased from the cart vendor.

"Monthly check-ins mean I actually miss our conversations," Sam said, handing Jordan a cup. "How's Chris doing?"

"Really well. We've been meeting weekly. He's going through the same struggles I did, but he's committed." Jordan sat down. "Last week he told me he made it through an entire team meeting without offering solutions. Just questions and reflection. Said it was the hardest forty-five minutes of his professional life."

Sam laughed. "Sounds familiar. What did you tell him?"

"That the discomfort means he's doing it right. That growth lives in the uncomfortable space." Jordan paused. "Actually, I've been thinking a lot about what to tell him next. About how to help him see the bigger picture of what he's building."

"What is the bigger picture?" Sam asked.

Jordan watched the river flow past, constant and patient. "It's about changing the fundamental relationship between leader and team. Moving from 'I have the answers' to 'We'll find the answers together.' From control to trust. From telling to asking."

"That's good," Sam said. "What else?"

"It's about listening. Really listening. Not just staying quiet while someone talks, but hearing what they're saying beneath the words. Listening for potential, not just performance. Listening for what people could become, not just what they can do for you right now."

Sam nodded slowly. "And what have you learned about listening over these past three months?"

Jordan thought about the question. About Sofia's exit interview where he'd finally heard what he'd been missing for years. About Taylor opening up when he reflected back her fear of losing her identity. About Devon lighting up when Jordan asked about his puzzles. About Kevin revealing capabilities Jordan had completely overlooked.

"I learned that listening is active, not passive," Jordan said. "It's work. It requires intention and presence. And it's the most powerful tool a leader has."

"Say more about that," Sam prompted.

"When you really listen to someone—when you're fully present and genuinely curious—you give them something most people rarely receive. You give them the experience of being truly heard. And that changes everything. It builds trust faster than any other technique. It unlocks thinking that stays locked when people feel like they're just being managed."

Jordan turned to face Sam directly. "You taught me to pause, to ask questions instead of providing answers, to reflect back what I hear, to be present. But underneath all of those techniques is one thing: learning to listen louder than I speak."

Sam's eyes brightened. "Listening louder. I like that phrase."

"It's the paradox you showed me on day one. The less you talk, the more influence you have. Because when you're quiet, you can actually hear. And when you hear, you can respond to what's really happening instead of what you assume is happening."

"The loudest leaders make noise," Sam said quietly. "The best leaders make space."

The words settled between them like a truth that had always existed, finally named.

"That's exactly it," Jordan said. "I spent years making noise—filling every silence with my ideas, my solutions, my thinking. I thought that's what leadership was. Being the loudest voice in the room."

"And now?"

"Now I know that leadership is about listening louder than anyone else. Hearing what people aren't saying. Creating space for voices that have been quiet because nobody made room for them. Making the quietest person in the meeting feel like their contribution matters as much as the loudest."

Sam pulled out his notebook—the same one he'd been using since their first meeting. He flipped back through pages filled with their conversations, their assignments, Jordan's struggles and breakthroughs.

"You know what's remarkable?" Sam said. "Three months ago, you came to me wanting techniques. Ways to fix your team's performance. Quick answers to immediate problems."

"I remember. You told me it wasn't about techniques. That it was about transformation."

"And you didn't really believe me. You thought if you could just learn the right skills, you could solve the problem." Sam smiled. "But what actually happened?"

Jordan considered the question. "I didn't learn skills. I unlearned habits. I didn't fix my team. I stopped breaking them. I didn't become a different leader. I became a different person."

"That's a transformation. Not adding new capabilities on top of old patterns. Fundamentally changing who you are and how you show up." Sam closed his notebook. "And here's what I want you to understand about what you've accomplished. You didn't just improve your team's performance. You created a ripple."

"A ripple?"

"Sofia left your team, but her departure became the catalyst for your transformation. The standard she described in that exit interview—what she needed from a leader—that's what you became. Taylor went from resistant to championing collaboration—she'll influence her future teams. Devon, Kevin, Marcus, Jamal—they've all experienced what it feels like when a leader actually listens. That experience changes what they'll accept from future leaders and what they'll do when they become leaders themselves."

Sam gestured to the river beside them. "You dropped a stone into the water by changing how you lead. But the ripples don't stop with your team. Chris is learning from you. The managers who heard you speak are questioning their own approaches. The ripple expands outward in ways you'll never fully see."

Jordan felt the weight and beauty of that truth. Leadership wasn't just about the team in front of you. It was about changing the culture one interaction at a time, one person at a time, one moment of genuine listening at a time.

"So, what comes next?" Jordan asked.

"You keep practicing. This isn't something you master and then stop doing. It's a practice, like meditation or exercise. Some days will be easier than others. You'll have moments where you slip back into old patterns—solving instead of asking, talking instead of listening. That's normal. The key is noticing when it happens and choosing differently next time."

"What about Chris? How long should I mentor him?"

"As long as he needs and you have capacity. But eventually, he'll be ready to mentor someone else. And you'll find another Chris. Or maybe you'll take on a bigger role in developing leaders across the organization." Sam paused. "The point is, this work doesn't end. You've discovered something valuable. Now you keep sharing it."

They sat in comfortable silence for a few minutes. The September sun felt warm but not oppressive. A couple walked past with a golden retriever who stopped to investigate the bench before being gently pulled along.

"Can I tell you something?" Jordan said. "I'm grateful for Sofia leaving. I know that sounds terrible, but it's true. If she hadn't quit, if that exit interview hadn't happened, I'd still be the old Jordan. Competent but limited. Hardworking but not developing anyone. I'd be making noise instead of space."

"That's not terrible. That's wisdom. Sometimes we need something to break before we can build it better." Sam stood up, shouldering his bag. "Our monthly check-ins can continue as long as you find them useful. But I suspect you're ready to run on your own now. You've internalized the principles. You're teaching them to others. That's when the student becomes the teacher."

Jordan stood as well. "I'd like to keep the monthly meetings if you're willing. Not because I need them, but because they help me stay grounded in the practice. Reflect on what's working and what isn't."

"Then monthly it is." Sam extended his hand. "I'm proud of who you've become, Jordan. Not just as a leader, but as a person. The work you've done is rare."

They shook hands, then embraced briefly. When Sam pulled back, his expression was knowing.

"Remember the question I asked you in our first meeting?" Sam said. "When did you last hear what someone wasn't saying?"

"I remember. I had no idea how to answer it."

"And now?"

Jordan thought about his conversation with Taylor that morning. She'd asked about taking on a mentorship role with a junior employee. But underneath her question was uncertainty about whether she was ready, whether Jordan thought she was capable. So he'd reflected back what he heard beneath the words, and Taylor had opened up about her fear of not being as good a mentor as she'd needed when she was junior.

"Now I hear what people aren't saying all the time," Jordan said. "Because I'm finally listening loudly enough to hear it."

Sam smiled. "That's how I know you've got this. Keep listening, Jordan. Keep making space. Keep showing others how to do the same."

He walked away along the riverside path, leaving Jordan standing by the bench where so much had changed over the past three months.

Jordan pulled out his phone and opened his notes app. He typed:

"Lessons from Sam:

- The loudest leaders make noise. The best leaders make space.

- Listening louder than you speak is the most powerful tool you have.

- Your silence gives others permission to think.

- Transformation isn't about adding skills. It's about unlearning habits.

- The ripple you create extends far beyond what you can see.

- This is a practice, not a destination. Keep practicing."

He saved the note and started walking back toward his car. Tomorrow was Friday, and his team had a big presentation to senior leadership about the account management system. Taylor and Kevin were leading it. Jordan's role was to introduce them and then stay quiet.

To listen.

To create space for their voices to be heard.

To practice what he'd learned about listening louder than he spoke.

The river flowed beside him, constant and patient, carving its path one small moment at a time.

Just like leadership.

Just like transformation.

Just like the quiet ripple that changed everything.

CHAPTER 18: LISTENING LOUDER

Several months had passed since that first desperate meeting with Sam.

Jordan arrived at the office on a Monday morning in late October, the fall air crisp and clean. Leaves scattered across the parking lot in shades of amber and gold. He walked through the familiar hallways with coffee in hand, nodding to colleagues, feeling the rhythm of a place he'd worked for years but understood differently now.

His calendar showed the usual Monday team meeting at nine. Nothing special about it. Just another week beginning.

Except for the email that had arrived over the weekend.

"Jordan - I hope this message finds you well. I wanted to reach out because I'm considering a move back to our company. My time at Meridian has been good, but I ran into Alex Martinez at an industry event and she mentioned your team has completely transformed. The way she described your leadership now—creating space for ideas, developing people—that's exactly what I was looking for. Would you be open to a conversation about returning? - Sofia"

Jordan had read the message three times, feeling something complicated settle in his chest. Pride that his transformation had been significant enough for people to notice. Regret that Sofia had experienced the worst of his leadership. Hope that maybe some things could be repaired.

He'd responded simply: "Sofia, I'd welcome the conversation. Let's talk this week."

Now, settling into his office before the team meeting, Jordan pulled up the latest performance data. His team's numbers over the past few months told a clear story:

Engagement: 89 (up from 72) Client satisfaction: 93 (up from 78) Revenue per employee: $394K (up from $287K) Project completion: 96% (up from 84%) Innovation index: 8.8 (up from 6.2)

All green. Top tier performance across every metric.

But the numbers weren't what made Jordan smile. It was the message thread in the team Slack channel from late Friday afternoon:

Devon: "Interesting challenge with the Patterson account. They want to accelerate timeline by three weeks. Thoughts?"

Kevin: "If we reallocate resources from the lower-priority projects, we could probably do it. But we'd need buy-in from those other clients on slight delays."

Taylor: "What if we brought in a contractor for the Patterson surge and kept our team on the original timeline? Might cost more but lower risk."

Marcus: "Or we could propose a phased delivery to Patterson. Give them the critical components in three weeks, the rest on the original timeline. They get what they need faster without us scrambling."

Jamal: "I like Marcus's idea. Let me draft a proposal and run it by Patterson tomorrow morning."

Devon: "Perfect. Let me know how it goes."

The entire conversation had happened without Jordan's involvement. A complex client challenge surfaced, discussed, solved, and actioned—all while he was enjoying his weekend.

That was the real transformation. Not that his team performed better, but that they performed independently oh him, but as a real team.

At 8:55, Jordan headed to Conference Room B. His team filed in over the next few minutes. Marcus, Taylor, Kevin, Devon, Jamal. Five people who looked nothing like the uncertain group from three months ago.

"Morning everyone," Jordan said. "Let's dive in. Three items today. First, the Patterson accelerated timeline Devon mentioned Friday. Jamal, you were going to talk to them?"

"I did, first thing this morning." Jamal pulled up his notes. "They loved Marcus's phased delivery idea. We're splitting it into two milestones—critical components delivered three weeks early, remaining features on the original schedule. They're actually happier with this than their original request because it reduces their risk too."

"Nice work," Jordan said. "What made you confident to pitch that instead of just accepting their timeline request?"

"Honestly? Listening to what they really needed versus what they asked for," Jamal said. "They kept saying 'we need to move faster,' but when I asked why, it was really about getting specific features to their board meeting. We didn't need to accelerate everything, just the pieces they needed to present."

Jordan noticed the language Jamal had used. Listening to what they really needed. The principles spreading through the team organically.

"Second item," Jordan continued. "Q4 planning. We need to set strategic priorities for the next three months. What are we seeing as the biggest opportunities or challenges?"

Taylor spoke first. "Client retention is strong, but we're not growing new accounts as aggressively as we could. I think we should focus on converting our best referrals into active clients."

"What would that take?" Jordan asked.

"Dedicated outreach capacity. Maybe we designate rotating team members to own new business development each month. That way it doesn't fall to the side when existing accounts get busy."

Kevin jumped in. "I like that. And we could use the client appreciation event model—interactive, collaborative sessions that show prospects how we work rather than just telling them."

"Resource implications?" Devon asked.

"Probably ten hours per week from whoever's on rotation," Taylor said. "But if we land even two new accounts per quarter, the ROI is massive."

Jordan watched the discussion unfold. People building on each other's ideas, asking substantive questions, thinking strategically. He'd contributed exactly two questions in five minutes of conversation.

The debate continued for another ten minutes. Jordan asked two more questions—"What are we not considering?" and "What would success look like?"—but otherwise stayed silent.

His team landed on a complete new business development plan without him solving a single piece of it.

"Third item," Jordan said, glancing at his watch. Twenty minutes into the meeting and they'd covered two major topics with genuine thinking and decision-making. "I want to give you all a heads up about a potential team addition. Sofia Reyes reached out about possibly returning to the company. I'm meeting with her this week to discuss it."

The room went quiet. Marcus and Taylor exchanged glances.

"How do we feel about that?" Jordan asked. "Be honest."

Marcus spoke carefully. "Sofia's talented. But she left because of... well, because things were different then."

"Because I was a different leader then," Jordan said directly. "You can say it."

"Right. So I guess the question is whether she'd fit with how we work now," Marcus said. "We're more collaborative, more autonomous. Would she want that, or would she expect the old dynamic?"

"Good question. What would help us evaluate that?" Jordan asked.

"Maybe she could sit in on a team meeting before we make any decisions?" Taylor suggested. "See if the culture fits what she's looking for now?"

"And we should be honest with her about how things have changed," Kevin added. "Make sure her expectations align with reality."

Jordan nodded. "I like both of those ideas. I'll propose them when we talk. Anything else we should consider?"

"Just that we've built something good here," Devon said quietly. "I'd want to make sure adding someone doesn't disrupt that. Even someone as talented as Sofia."

"Agreed," Jordan said. "The team culture we've built is worth protecting. We'll be thoughtful about this."

The meeting wrapped at 9:35. Thirty-five minutes, three substantial topics, complete ownership from the team.

Jordan had spoken maybe ten percent of the total words in the room.

And it had been the most productive meeting of the week.

Wednesday afternoon, Jordan met Sofia at the same coffee shop where he'd first met with Alex. She looked the same—professional, composed, confident. But her expression was more open than he remembered from their working relationship.

"Thanks for meeting," Sofia said as they settled at a table. "I know this might be awkward."

"It doesn't have to be," Jordan said. "I'm glad you reached out. Tell me about your time at Meridian."

Sofia described the past several months. Good projects, smart colleagues, competitive salary. But something was missing.

"The culture there is very top-down," she explained. "I thought I wanted a place that would value my strategic thinking, but it turns out they just want me to execute their strategy, not contribute to it. Different cage, same limitations."

Jordan paused, letting her words settle. "What made you think about coming back here?"

"I ran into Alex Martinez at an industry event last month. She mentioned that your team had completely transformed. That you'd become one of the best leaders in the company." Sofia looked at him directly. "That surprised me. So I asked around. Talked to some people who'd worked with your team recently. They all said the same thing—Jordan's team is different now. Collaborative, engaged. The kind of environment I wish I'd had when I was there."

"You deserved that environment," Jordan said. "I'm sorry I didn't create it when you were on the team."

Sofia seemed taken aback by the direct apology. "I appreciate you saying that."

"It's true. You brought me excellent thinking, and I consistently redirected you toward my own ideas. I made you feel like an assistant instead of a contributor. That exit interview you gave was painful to hear, but it was also the wake-up call I needed."

They talked for an hour. Jordan described his transformation honestly—the mentorship with Sam, the uncomfortable learning process, the gradual shift in how his team operated. He didn't oversell or make promises. Just described reality.

"Here's what I want you to know," Jordan said. "If you come back, it will be genuinely different. But different means you'll have more autonomy and more responsibility. You'll be expected to think strategically, make decisions, sometimes fail and learn from it. I won't solve problems for you—I'll help you develop the capability to solve them yourself."

"That's exactly what I want," Sofia said.

"The team would want to meet with you first. Make sure the fit works both ways. Are you comfortable with that?"

"Absolutely."

"Then let's set that up. No promises either direction, just a conversation." Jordan paused. "And Sofia, if this doesn't work out, if you decide this isn't the right move or we decide it's not the right fit—that's okay too. I genuinely want you to end up somewhere you can thrive, whether that's here or somewhere else."

Sofia smiled. "You really have changed."

Friday morning, Sofia sat in on the team meeting. Jordan watched his team engage with her—asking about her experience at Meridian, describing how they worked now, being honest about both the opportunities and the challenges of their collaborative approach.

Afterward, the team met privately to discuss.

"I vote yes," Taylor said. "She asked great questions and seemed genuinely excited about how we work now."

"Agreed," Marcus added. "And having someone with her experience would help us tackle bigger strategic projects."

The rest of the team nodded agreement.

Sofia accepted the offer that afternoon.

Late Friday, after everyone had left, Jordan sat in his quiet office and pulled out his phone. A text from Chris had come through an hour earlier:

"Had my first real breakthrough today. A team member brought me a challenge they were facing, and I started asking questions until she solved it herself. She looked so proud when she figured it out. This is amazing."

Jordan smiled and typed back: "That's the moment that makes it all worth it. Proud of you."

Then he opened a new message and wrote:

"Chris - For week one of next month, try this: say nothing for the first ten minutes of your next team meeting. Just listen. Watch what happens when you create that much space. Then call me and tell me what you learned."

He hit send and opened his laptop. He had an email draft he'd been working on to David Chen, proposing a leadership development program for mid-level managers across the company. Teaching them what he'd learned about listening, about creating space, about developing people instead of directing them.

The loudest leaders make noise. The best leaders make space.

He'd lived both versions. He knew which one actually worked.

Outside his window, the October sunset painted the sky in shades of orange and purple. The parking lot had emptied except for a few cars and the building had gone quiet.

Jordan thought about the journey from that Monday morning three months ago—checking his phone during a team meeting, jumping in with solutions after thirty seconds, losing Sofia because he'd never truly heard her.

To now. A team that solved problems independently. Engagement scores in the top tier. Sofia choosing to return because the culture had changed so fundamentally.

The irony wasn't lost on him. His office was quieter now than it had ever been. He spent less time solving and more time listening. His calendar had more white space because his team needed less of his time.

And yet the results were louder than they'd ever been.

That was the paradox Sam had tried to teach him from day one. The less you talk, the more influence you have. Your silence gives others permission to find their answers.

Listening louder than you speak.

Jordan closed his laptop and stood to leave. Monday would bring new challenges, new opportunities to practice what he'd learned. He also thought about how Sofia's first day back in a couple of weeks would be interesting—seeing the team through her eyes, navigating the transition, ensuring she felt genuinely included in the new dynamic.

But he wasn't worried. His team knew how to handle complexity now. They'd figure it out together.

Because that's what teams did when their leader created space instead of filling it.

When their leader listened louder than they spoke.

Jordan turned off his office light and headed home, carrying with him the quiet confidence of someone who'd learned that the most powerful thing a leader could do was often the hardest thing:

Stop talking.

Start listening.

And trust that the space between would fill itself with thinking better than anything you could have provided alone.

The loudest leaders make noise.

The best leaders make space.

And somewhere in that space, if you listened closely enough, you could hear the sound of people becoming more than they ever thought possible.

THE LISTENING LOUDER FRAMEWORK

A Practical Guide to Implementation

Jordan's transformation wasn't magic.
It was the consistent application of ten principles.
This framework gives you the same roadmap.

WHAT'S INSIDE

THE 10 PRINCIPLES:

1. The Listening Paradox
2. The 3-Second Pause
3. Ask, Don't Tell
4. Listen for Potential
5. The Echo Effect (Reflection)
6. Presence as Productivity
7. Discomfort Is the Job
8. The Trust Compound Effect
9. Development Over Direction
10. Listen Louder Than You Speak

IMPLEMENTATION TOOLS:

- Quick Reference Cheat Sheet
- 30-Day Implementation Guide
- Self-Assessment Tool

PRINCIPLE 1

The Listening Paradox

WHAT IT IS

Leaders who talk the least often achieve the most. The less you speak, the more influence you create. Your silence gives your team permission to think, grow, and own solutions.

WHY IT MATTERS

When you dominate conversations, you develop yourself but stunt your team. When you create space, you develop leaders. Jordan talked 70% of the time and got mediocre results. When he reduced talk time to 10%, engagement jumped from 72% to 89%.

HOW TO APPLY IT

- Track your talk time in your next three meetings
- Set a goal: speak less than 30% of the time
- When you catch yourself about to solve a problem, pause and ask a question instead
- Count how many questions you ask vs. statements you make

KEY QUESTION

Am I creating space for thinking, or am I filling it with my own thoughts?

COMMON PITFALL

Believing that silence means you're not adding value. Your silence IS the value—it's the space where your team's thinking develops.

YOU'LL KNOW IT'S WORKING WHEN

Team members start bringing you solutions instead of problems. Meetings become more energized even though you're speaking less. People stop waiting for your opinion before sharing theirs.

PRINCIPLE 2

The 3-Second Pause

WHAT IT IS

The space between hearing and responding. Most people respond in
0.2 seconds—they're not listening, they're waiting to talk. Real
listening requires a three-second pause to process before
responding.

WHY IT MATTERS

The pause is where wisdom lives. It's the difference between
reacting and responding. In those three seconds, you process what
was actually said, notice what wasn't said, and craft a response that
serves the other person instead of just satisfying your own need to
speak.

HOW TO APPLY IT

- After someone finishes speaking, silently count: "one-
  thousand-one, one-thousand-two, one-thousand-three"
- Use the pause to ask yourself: "What did they really
  mean?"
- If the silence feels awkward, that's normal—sit in it
- Notice how often people keep talking when you don't
  immediately respond

KEY QUESTION

*Am I responding to what they said, or reacting to what I think they
meant?*

COMMON PITFALL

Filling the silence because it feels uncomfortable. The discomfort is part of the process. Your comfort with silence teaches your team that thinking time is valued.

YOU'LL KNOW IT'S WORKING WHEN

People start adding more detail after you pause—they interpret your silence as interest. Your responses become more insightful. You stop saying things you immediately regret.

PRINCIPLE 3

Ask, Don't Tell

WHAT IT IS

Leading through questions instead of answers. Helping people find solutions rather than handing them solutions. Using the question pyramid: start broad (open), narrow down (focused), confirm understanding (closed).

WHY IT MATTERS

When you give answers, people become dependent. When you ask questions, people become capable. Solutions they discover stick better than solutions you assign. Ownership comes from authorship.

HOW TO APPLY IT

- Start with: "What do you think we should do?"
- Follow with: "What else?" (at least three times)
- Challenge yourself: Can I ask one more question before giving an answer?
- Practice the pyramid: Open → Focused → Closed
  - Example: "What's your take?" → "What would success look like?" → "So you're thinking we should X?"

KEY QUESTION

Am I asking because I'm curious, or because I already know the answer I want?

COMMON PITFALL

Asking leading questions—questions that manipulate people toward your predetermined answer. Genuine questions have no hidden agenda. You're truly curious about their thinking.

YOU'LL KNOW IT'S WORKING WHEN

People come to you with solutions, not just problems. Team members say "I figured it out" instead of "You told me what to do." Decisions get implemented faster because people own them.

PRINCIPLE 4

Listen for Potential

WHAT IT IS

Listening for who someone could become, not just what they're saying right now. Using the "Three Potentials" framework: listen for capability (what they're naturally good at), growth (what they're curious about), and contribution (what they care about).

WHY IT MATTERS

Most managers listen to assess current performance. Great leaders listen to unlock future potential. Kevin seemed "adequate" until Jordan listened for his systems thinking. Taylor seemed like "just an executor" until Jordan heard her strategic mind. People rise or fall to the ceiling you set for them with your listening.

HOW TO APPLY IT

- Ask yourself: What capability is this person showing that they might not see in themselves?
- Listen for: "What energizes them when they talk?" That's where potential lives
- Notice: When does their voice change or eyes light up? Those are clues
- Apply the Three Potentials:
    1. CAPABILITY: What are they naturally good at?
    2. GROWTH: What are they curious about?
    3. CONTRIBUTION: What do they care about?
- The gap between where they are and where they could be = your leadership opportunity

KEY QUESTION

Am I listening to who they are now, or who they could become?

COMMON PITFALL

Categorizing people early and stopping paying attention to anything that doesn't fit that category. "Kevin is the quiet guy who executes tasks" becomes a cage that prevents you from seeing his strategic capability.

YOU'LL KNOW IT'S WORKING WHEN

Team members surprise you with capabilities you didn't know they had. People grow into bigger roles. Someone you wrote off as "adequate" becomes exceptional when you create space for their potential to emerge.

PRINCIPLE 5

The Echo Effect (Reflection)

WHAT IT IS

Reflecting back what you heard—not word-for-word repetition, but paraphrasing the meaning, emotion, and thing beneath their words. Showing the person you actually heard them before moving to problem-solving or your own response.

WHY IT MATTERS

Most people go through life without feeling truly heard. When you reflect back accurately, something shifts. They feel understood. And that understanding creates trust faster than almost anything else. Taylor opened up about her fear of change only after Jordan showed he understood her grief over losing her "executor" identity.

HOW TO APPLY IT

- After someone shares something important, pause and say: "So what I'm hearing is..."
- Paraphrase their meaning, not just their words
- Include the emotion: "It sounds like you're feeling..."
- Check: "Is that right? Am I understanding you correctly?"
- Don't jump to solutions—just reflect first

KEY QUESTION

Am I showing them I heard them, or am I just waiting to respond with my own thoughts?

COMMON PITFALL

Skipping reflection and jumping straight to problem-solving. When someone shares a concern and you immediately offer a solution, they don't feel heard—they feel managed.

YOU'LL KNOW IT'S WORKING WHEN

People say "Yes, exactly!" when you reflect. Defensive people become open. Resistant people become willing to try. Trust builds faster than you expected.

PRINCIPLE 6

Presence as Productivity

WHAT IT IS

Being fully engaged with what's happening right now—mentally, emotionally, and physically present. Not planning your response, not thinking about your next meeting, not checking your phone. All of you engaged with the person or task in front of you.

WHY IT MATTERS

The highest form of productivity isn't getting more done. It's being fully engaged with what you're doing. When you're present—truly present—the quality of everything improves. Your questions get sharper. Your listening gets deeper. Your decisions get wiser. Your relationships get stronger.

HOW TO APPLY IT

- In one-on-ones: Close laptop, silence phone, put it out of sight
- Clear your mind of what you were just working on before someone walks in
- For that person, for those 20-30 minutes, nothing else exists
- Notice when your mind wanders—don't judge it, just gently bring yourself back
- Practice this sentence: "Let me close out what I'm doing so I can give you my full attention"
-

KEY QUESTION

Am I physically here but mentally somewhere else?

COMMON PITFALL

Confusing constant availability with productivity. Being partially available to everything means being fully available to nothing. Your divided attention doesn't help anyone.

YOU'LL KNOW IT'S WORKING WHEN

People remember conversations with you differently—"You made me feel like I was the most important thing in the world." You notice more—expressions, tone, what's not being said. You arrive at the end of meetings more centered, not more fragmented.

PRINCIPLE 7

Discomfort Is the Job

WHAT IT IS

Growth lives in discomfort—for you and for your team. The awkward silence, the uncertainty of not having immediate answers, the vulnerability of admitting you don't know, the tension of watching someone struggle when you could solve it in seconds. That discomfort isn't a problem to fix. It's the work.

WHY IT MATTERS

When you eliminate discomfort, you eliminate growth. Jordan's team felt uncomfortable when he stopped giving them all the answers. Taylor resisted because the new way felt scary. But that discomfort was them growing. When you try to make everyone comfortable, you keep everyone small.

HOW TO APPLY IT

- When silence gets awkward, count to ten before filling it
- When someone struggles with a problem you could solve, ask one more question instead
- When you feel uncertain, name it: "I don't have the answer, and that's okay"
- When your team pushes back on change, acknowledge the discomfort without eliminating it
- Remember: Your job isn't to make everyone comfortable. It's to help everyone grow.

KEY QUESTION

Am I trying to eliminate discomfort, or am I normalizing it as part of growth?

COMMON PITFALL

Mistaking discomfort for dysfunction. When people resist your new approach, it doesn't mean the approach is wrong—it means they're in the learning zone. Discomfort means it's working.

YOU'LL KNOW IT'S WORKING WHEN

You get comfortable being uncomfortable. Your team stops expecting you to have all the answers. People work through problems themselves even when it's hard. Growth becomes normal, not exceptional.

PRINCIPLE 8

The Trust Compound Effect

WHAT IT IS

Trust doesn't build linearly—it compounds. Like financial investments, early deposits show little return. For weeks or months, nothing seems to change. Then suddenly, exponential growth. Jordan worked with Sam for six weeks before seeing results. Then everything shifted at once.

WHY IT MATTERS

Most leaders give up during the flat period. They make deposits—asking questions, creating space, listening deeply—and see no change. So they go back to the old way. But trust is compounding in the background. You just can't see it yet. The question isn't "Is this working?" The question is "Am I making consistent deposits?"

HOW TO APPLY IT

- Commit to a timeline before evaluating results: minimum 6-8 weeks
- Track deposits, not just outcomes: Did I pause? Did I ask? Did I listen?
- Expect the flat period—plan for it mentally
- When you're tempted to go back to the old way, make one more deposit instead
- Trust the compound curve: slow start, exponential finish

KEY QUESTION

Am I making consistent deposits, or am I only measuring immediate returns?

COMMON PITFALL

Giving up during the flat period. "This isn't working" really means "The results haven't compounded yet." Stay consistent through the slow start.

YOU'LL KNOW IT'S WORKING WHEN

After weeks of small changes, suddenly everything shifts at once. Team members who were skeptical become advocates. Performance jumps. Culture changes. The compound effect pays off exponentially.

PRINCIPLE 9

Development Over Direction

WHAT IT IS

Choosing to develop people's capability instead of just directing their work. Asking "What do you think?" even when it would be faster to just tell them. Creating leaders, not executors. Building capacity, not just completing tasks.

WHY IT MATTERS

Direction creates short-term efficiency but long-term dependency. Development creates short-term investment but long-term capability. Every time you solve a problem, you get better at solving it but your team stays the same. Every time you help them solve it, they get better and you multiply your impact.

HOW TO APPLY IT

- Ask yourself: "Am I solving this problem, or am I developing someone's capability to solve it?"
- Default to questions: "What do you think we should do?" before giving answers
- When tempted to take over a task, pause and ask: "What would help you succeed with this?"
- Celebrate capability development, not just task completion
- Measure: How many people can now do things without me that they couldn't do three months ago?

KEY QUESTION

Am I building my capacity or their capacity?

COMMON PITFALL

Choosing efficiency over development because it feels faster. It is faster—today. But you'll pay the cost of dependency forever. Development is an investment that pays exponential returns.

YOU'LL KNOW IT'S WORKING WHEN

Your team solves problems without involving you. People you developed get promoted. New challenges don't overwhelm you because your team has grown in capability. You become the leader who develops other leaders.

PRINCIPLE 10

Listen Louder Than You Speak

WHAT IT IS

The culmination of all nine principles. Making your listening—your attention, your questions, your presence, your development of others—louder than your own voice. Creating more influence through silence than through speech.

WHY IT MATTERS

This is the paradox that changes everything. In a world where everyone is shouting for attention, your listening is what makes people feel heard. In organizations drowning in direction, your questions are what create ownership. In teams craving development, your silence is what creates space for growth.

HOW TO APPLY IT

- Practice all nine principles consistently
- Track this metric: In meetings, who talked more—you or your team?
- Aim for: Your talk time = 10-30%, Team talk time = 70-90%
- Ask yourself daily: "Did I create more value through my questions or my answers today?"
- Remember: Influence grows as volume decreases

KEY QUESTION

What am I saying with my silence that my words never could?

COMMON PITFALL

Believing that your value comes from having answers. Your value comes from developing others' capability to find answers. That's leadership.

YOU'LL KNOW IT'S WORKING WHEN

You walk out of meetings having barely spoken, and they were the most productive meetings of the week. Your team describes you as their best boss not because you were the smartest, but because you made them smarter. People want to work for you because they know they'll grow.

QUICK REFERENCE CHEAT SHEET

THE 10 PRINCIPLES AT A GLANCE

#	PRINCIPLE	CORE PRACTICE	KEY QUESTION
1	Listening Paradox	Talk less, influence more	Am I creating space or filling it?
2	3-Second Pause	Count to 3 before responding	Am I responding or reacting?
3	Ask, Don't Tell	Questions over answers	Am I curious or manipulating?
4	Listen for Potential	Hear who they could become	Do I see potential or just performance?
5	Echo Effect	Reflect before solving	Am I showing I heard them?
6	Presence as Productivity	Be fully where you are	Am I mentally here?
7	Discomfort Is the Job	Growth lives in awkwardness	Am I normalizing discomfort?
8	Trust Compound	Consistent deposits pay off	Am I making deposits or measuring returns?
9	Development Over Direction	Build capability, not dependency	Am I developing or just directing?
10	Listen Louder	Silence creates influence	What am I saying with my silence?

30-DAY IMPLEMENTATION GUIDE

WEEK 1: THE FOUNDATION

Focus: Principles 1-2 (Paradox & Pause)

DAILY PRACTICE:

- **Day 1-2:** Track your talk time in every meeting. Just observe, don't change anything yet.
- **Day 3-5:** Practice the 3-second pause in every conversation. Try to count it out mentally.
- **Day 6-7:** Combine them: Pause for 3 seconds, then respond with a question instead of an answer.

REFLECTION QUESTIONS:

- What percentage of meeting time did I spend talking?
- How often did I fill silence instead of sitting in it?
- When I paused, what did I notice that I would have missed?

WEEK 2: THE QUESTIONS

Focus: Principle 3 (Ask, Don't Tell)

DAILY PRACTICE:

- **Day 8-10:** Start every response with: "What do you think we should do?"
- **Day 11-12:** Practice "What else?" at least 3 times in each conversation
- **Day 13-14:** Use the question pyramid (Open → Focused → Closed) in one-on-ones

REFLECTION QUESTIONS:

- How many times did I solve a problem vs. ask a question?
- When people answered my questions, did they own the solution?
- What happened when I asked "What else?" three times?

WEEK 3: THE DEPTH

Focus: Principles 4-5 (Potential & Echo)

DAILY PRACTICE:

- **Day 15-17:** Apply "Three Potentials" framework with each team member
    - What capability am I seeing?
    - What are they curious about?
    - What do they care about?
- **Day 18-21:** Practice reflection: "So what I'm hearing is..." before responding

REFLECTION QUESTIONS:

- What potential did I discover that I had missed before?
- When I reflected back, how did people respond?
- Who surprised me this week with capability I hadn't seen?

WEEK 4: THE COMMITMENT

Focus: Principles 6-10 (Presence, Discomfort, Trust, Development, Listen Louder)

DAILY PRACTICE:

- **Day 22-24:** Full presence practice
    - Close laptop in one-on-ones
    - Put phone out of sight
    - Be fully where you are
- **Day 25-27:** Sit in discomfort
    - Don't fill awkward silences
    - Watch people struggle without rescuing them
    - Trust the process
- **Day 28-30:** Integration
    - Apply all 10 principles
    - Track your listening vs. talking ratio
    - Notice what's different

REFLECTION QUESTIONS:

- How did full presence change my conversations?
- When I sat in discomfort, what emerged?
- What's different in my team after 30 days?

AFTER 30 DAYS: ASSESS YOUR PROGRESS

Use the Self-Assessment Tool (next section) to measure:

- Has your talk time decreased?
- Are team members bringing more solutions?
- Is trust building?
- Are people growing in capability?

Then recommit for another 30 days.

The compound effect doesn't stop at 30 days—it accelerates.

SELF-ASSESSMENT TOOL

LISTENING LOUDER ASSESSMENT

Rate yourself honestly (1 = Never, 5 = Always)

THE LISTENING PARADOX

- In meetings, I speak less than 30% of the time
- Team members bring me solutions, not just problems
- I'm comfortable with silence in conversations
- People share their thinking without prompting **SCORE: ___ / 20**

THE 3-SECOND PAUSE

- I count to 3 before responding in conversations
- I process what was said before formulating my response
- I notice what wasn't said, not just what was said
- My responses are thoughtful, not reactive **SCORE: ___ / 20**

ASK, DON'T TELL

- My first response to problems is "What do you think?"
- I ask "What else?" at least 3 times in important conversations
- Team members own the solutions they propose
- I'm genuinely curious about their thinking **SCORE: ___ / 20**

LISTEN FOR POTENTIAL

- I notice capability in people they don't see in themselves
- I apply the Three Potentials framework regularly
- People surprise me with hidden talents
- I see the gap between who they are and who they could be
  SCORE: ___ / 20

THE ECHO EFFECT

- I reflect back what I heard before problem-solving
- People say "Yes, exactly!" when I paraphrase
- I show understanding before offering solutions
- Trust builds quickly in my relationships **SCORE: ___ / 20**

PRESENCE AS PRODUCTIVITY

- I close my laptop and put my phone away in one-on-ones
- I'm fully engaged in conversations, not planning my response
- People feel like they're my top priority when we talk
- I notice subtle cues (tone, expression, energy) **SCORE: ___ / 20**

DISCOMFORT IS THE JOB

- I sit in awkward silences instead of filling them
- I watch people struggle without rescuing them immediately
- I normalize discomfort as part of growth
- I'm comfortable not having all the answers **SCORE: ___ / 20**

TRUST COMPOUND EFFECT

- I make consistent "trust deposits" even without immediate results
- I commit to approaches for 6-8 weeks before evaluating

- I track behaviors (deposits) not just outcomes
- I trust the compound curve through slow starts **SCORE: ___ / 20**

DEVELOPMENT OVER DIRECTION

- I develop capability instead of just completing tasks
- I measure: How many people can do things without me now?
- I choose development even when direction would be faster
- My team is growing in capability, not just executing **SCORE: ___ / 20**

LISTEN LOUDER THAN YOU SPEAK

- My influence comes more from questions than answers
- My team talks 70-90% of the time in meetings
- People describe me as someone who made them smarter
- My silence creates more value than my words **SCORE: ___ / 20**

YOUR TOTAL SCORE: ___ / 200

180-200: You're listening louder! Keep practicing and deepening. **140-179:** Strong foundation. Focus on your lowest-scored principles. **100-139:** Good start. Pick 2-3 principles to focus on this month. **60-99:** Significant opportunity. Start with Week 1 of the 30-Day Guide. **Below 60:** You're exactly where Jordan was. The transformation starts now.

PROGRESS TRACKER

Re-take this assessment every 30 days:

Date Total Score Top 3 Strengths Top 3 Growth Areas

_______ _______ _______________ _______________

_______ _______ _______________ _______________

_______ _______ _______________ _______________

_______ _______ _______________ _______________

What to track:

- Your total score (expect it to dip before it rises—discomfort is growth!)
- Which principles improved most
- Which principles still need focus
- Specific examples of success

FINAL THOUGHT

"The leader who talks the most often listens the least."

Jordan's transformation took 3 months of consistent practice. Not because the principles are complicated—they're simple. But because applying them requires unlearning decades of habits.

This framework doesn't make the work easier.

It makes the work clearer.

You know what to do. Now do it.

Listen louder than you speak.

And watch what becomes possible.

The End

ACKNOWLEDGMENTS

Over the years I have had the privilege to learn from many great leaders (and some not so great) who have taught me the value of listening. Not just hearing, but really listening. In addition, there are several people who contributed their time assisting with the final version of this book and without them, this would not have been possible. I would like to acknowledge the following people:

Kristen Greig, for always believing in me.

Julie Tally – for the honest and extremely helpful feedback on this book. Your insight was truly valuable.

For more resources, visit www.joelgreig.com or connect on LinkedIn @joelgreig.

About the Author

Joel Greig brings over 25 years of leadership experience from the real estate development and property management industry, where he's worked with some of the world's leading companies managing multi-million dollar portfolios and teams across several US markets, including New York City, Boston and San Diego.

His career taught him a counter-intuitive truth: the leaders who talked the least often achieved the most.

Today, as a personal coach, author, and speaker, Joel helps leaders make the shift from directing to developing. Listening Louder is his second book.

He lives in Oceanside, California.

9 798994 855515